men MINISTRY

in the 21st century

the encyclopedia of practical ideas

Bible studies
retreats
guys movie nights

reaching men

Group

Loveland, Colorado

www.grouppublishing.com

Group resources actually work!

This Group resource helps you focus on **"The 1 Thing™"**— a life-changing relationship with Jesus Christ. "The 1 Thing" incorporates our **R.E.A.L.** approach to ministry. It reinforces a growing friendship with Jesus, encourages long-term learning, and results in life transformation, because it's:

Relational
Learner-to-learner interaction enhances learning and builds Christian friendships.

Experiential
What learners experience through discussion and action sticks with them up to 9 times longer than what they simply hear or read.

Applicable
The aim of Christian education is to equip learners to be both hearers and doers of God's Word.

Learner-based
Learners understand and retain more when the learning process takes into consideration how they learn best.

Men s Ministry in the 21st Century: The Encyclopedia of Practical Ideas
Copyright ' 2004 Group Publishing, Inc.

Visit our Web site: **www.grouppublishing.com**

Credits
Editor: Brad Lewis
Creative Development Editor: Matt Lockhart
Chief Creative Officer: Joani Schultz
Art Director: Granite Design
Print Production Artist: Granite Design
Cover Art Director: Jeff A. Storm
Cover Design: Toolbox Creative
Illustration: Rex Bohn
Photos: Photodisc
Production Manager: Peggy Naylor

Unless otherwise noted, Scripture taken from the HOLY BIBLE, NEW INTERNATIONAL VERSION¤. Copyright ' 1973, 1978, 1984 by International Bible Society. Used by permission of Zondervan Publishing House. All rights reserved.

Library of Congress Cataloging-in-Publication Data
Men's ministry in the 21st century : the encyclopedia of practical
ideas.-- 1st American pbk. ed.
      p. cm.
   ISBN 0-7644-2699-0 (pbk. : alk. paper)
   1. Church work with men. I. Group Publishing.
   BV4440.M46 2004
   259'.081--dc22

                                                    20040066

20

10 9 8 7 6 5 4 3 2 1   13 12 11 10 09 08 07 06 05 04
Printed in the United States of America.

Contents

Section 3—Get Men to Care About Each Other

5. Relationship Building: Beyond "I'm Fine, How Are You?"

6. Bible Studies: Into the Word and Each Other's Lives

Toolbox

Section 4—Get Men to Reach Out

8. Outreach: Stepping Out of Your Comfort Zone

What Is Outreach?

Ten Key Values for Men's Outreach

Training and Equipping for Outreach

Nineteen Steps to a Life-Changing Outreach Event

Challenge

Toolbox

Introduction

Welcome to *Men's Ministry in the 21st Century: The Encyclopedia of Practical Ideas.*

Hmm…men's ministry. Interestingly, when it comes to most of the groups in your church—children, youth, singles, women, senior adults—you could start or grow a ministry by going wild with fun new activities and events. But when it comes to ministering to and with the men in your church, things are a little different.

Why?

Well, guys tend to be different. For example, when it comes to their relationships with other guys at church, they often don't go much deeper than a handshake or a slap on the back and some superficial shooting of the breeze in the foyer on Sunday mornings.

That's fine. Until trouble strikes a man and his family. Then, because he hasn't formed any decent relationships with other guys, he doesn't have a friend to turn to when he's dealing with the consequences of a bad choice, going through trouble with his teenager, dealing with the death of a parent, or facing any other problem that just comes with life.

So that's the underlying theme of this book. Yes, it's chock-full of tools, activities, events, and nuts and bolts about how you can start and build a ministry to and with men in your church. Some of these things are hard work, others are just fun. Some are meaningful and inspirational, others are merely practical and functional. Some are intensely spiritual and life-transforming, others are simply ideas to help men test the waters of getting involved.

To provide all of that, we've pulled together some of the best guys we could find. But all of our contributors—many who've been involved in men's ministry for years—realize that *without* drawing men in and connecting all the tools, activities, events, and nuts and bolts to the purpose of helping guys form and deepen relationships with each other and with God, the resulting ministry will be empty.

God passionately loves men. He desires that men keenly love him. God wants to use men. He wants men to serve him, their wives, their families, and others in significant and meaningful ways.

Our prayer as you use this book is that—beyond your wildest expectations—God will bless you, the guys in your church, those you reach out to beyond the walls of your church, and the lives that together you'll change for eternity.

—Brad Lewis, Editor

Section 1
GET STARTED

Chapter 1

Why Men's Ministry? It's All About Relationships

by Steve Sonderman

Chapter summary: Throw out your old ways of thinking, and use these new building blocks for ministry to men in the twenty-first century.

Chapter 2

Leadership Team: Winning the Battle to Find Great Leaders

by Gentry Gardner

Chapter summary: Practical steps and tools that you can use for building your men's ministry leadership team.

WHY MEN'S MINISTRY? IT'S ALL ABOUT RELATIONSHIPS

When you hear the words *men's ministry,* what comes to mind? My guess is that you conjure up images of a Saturday morning breakfast in the basement of the church with a dozen or so men who've been around since Moses. They're eating food that will clog your arteries faster than glue. The conversation centers around what they shot on their last round of golf and how the local sports teams are doing.

Over the years, we've put men's ministry in a box. We think of ushering, golf outings, retreats, men's small groups, T-bones and steak fries, and an assortment of other activities and events. Not that any one of these activities is wrong or bad. But sadly, they've kept us from truly ministering to the men of our churches. We've settled for much less than what an effective ministry to men could really be. It's time for a change. Let's blow open the box men's ministry gets placed in and open our eyes to the potential of what men's ministry can be in the church.

Let's start by getting rid of some of the false caricatures of what men's ministry is, discuss some of the problems common in men's ministries, and lay the foundational blocks for ministry to men.

Before we begin, I need to tell you two things right from the start.

1. There's no greater joy than working with the men of your church. I've been involved with the men at Elmbrook Church for the past ten years, and I've thoroughly enjoyed every minute of it. Of course, we've been through difficult times and long hours, but those pale in comparison to the fulfillment that comes from seeing men's lives transformed, marriages restored, relationships healed, addictions broken, friendships formed, and workers for the harvest developed.

2. There's no quick way to do men's ministry. It takes time to do it right. The process of dreaming about and starting a men's ministry will likely take several years for you to implement. The good news is that what you do will result in a life-changing men's ministry in your church.

What Is Men's Ministry?

I believe that when you get down to the nitty-gritty, men's ministry is one thing: One man walking with another man, helping him to know Christ in a deeper way. Notice that my definition doesn't mention activities or events. Men's ministry doesn't depend on the size of your church or leadership team. It doesn't involve a bigger program, better strategy, or a brilliant leader.

It involves a relationship—one man with another.

Relationship is something that anyone can do. If you attend a church with one hundred members, forty of which are men—about the average-sized church in America—your ministry may look like this: You call up one of the men in your church and ask him to have lunch this week. At lunch you ask how things are going in his marriage, at work, with his kids, and between him and the Lord. Don't be surprised if he pours out his heart to you. Your job is simple—listen, draw him out, love him, encourage him, and commit to pray for him. Whether you know it or not, you're doing men's ministry! The next week you call another guy and ask him to meet you for breakfast and do the exact same thing. If you met with one man from your congregation each week of the year, you'd have an incredible ministry. Notice that we haven't even mentioned mission statements, retreats, or Saturday breakfasts. Yet you'd be making a huge impact for the kingdom of God!

Let's look at another church. Maybe you come from a church of two hundred. You call up three men and ask them to meet an hour each week for Bible study and prayer. For a year you pour your life into them. You ground them in the basics of Christianity, help them discover their role in the church, and give them a vision of multiplication. When the year's up, you encourage each of them to find three other men and do the same thing. You now have four groups of men meeting in your church. This is also men's ministry, and it's just as significant as any programmed event. You're helping men grow into fully devoted followers of Jesus.

If you're in a church of 750 to 1,000, your ministry to men may look different. You may want to find three to eight other men who have a vision for ministering to men, then spend the next year together studying, praying, and discussing how you're going to reach the men of your church.

I hope you get the idea. Men's ministry isn't about big programs and a lot of meetings; it's about one man investing his life in another. The size of your church, budget, and staff doesn't really make a difference. What it comes down to is a willingness to get close to another man, walk with him through life, and allow God to make him into the man God wants him to be.

Problems With Men's Ministry

Over the past ten years, I've consulted with thousands of leaders on how to start men's ministry in the local church. Through all these interactions, I've run across a number of common problems. Allow me to lay these out and provide a quick explanation of what you can do to avoid these problems in your church.

■ Led by One

One common scenario is when a man comes home from a men's conference or event and he's excited to start something at his church. As men, most of us have the propensity "to do something." So this man starts with what comes naturally—he plans an event. When that goes well, the men in his church want more, so he starts a small group, then a retreat, and then a service project. The list goes on and on. Unfortunately, one guy is doing it all. He's never taken the time to develop a team of men to carry the ball with him. So when he burns out, gets transferred, or has a vision for another ministry, the men's ministry comes to a screeching halt.

The answer seems obvious on paper. An effective ministry needs to be based on a team approach rather than on an individual. While one person may have the initial vision and passion, he must develop a team of men around him to make men's ministry happen. This team allows more men to use their gifts, encourage each other, and get more done.

■ Based Only on Activities and Events

Often when I ask a leader about the men's ministry in his church, he quickly lists all the events they've held in the past year. His eyes light up, his chest sticks out, and he's very proud of all they're doing. The events get bigger and better—bigger-name speakers, bigger-name bands, and bigger steaks! Unfortunately, when a ministry is based only on events and activities, it doesn't take long for men to stop showing up. They've "been there, done that, have the T-shirt."

The solution is to develop a ministry based on relationships rather than activity. The result is that men will come together not to hear another speaker or celebrity's testimony but because of the relationships they're developing with other men. Who you stick up front isn't the draw. Of course, all this takes time.

I want to add that events and activities certainly do have a place in effective ministry to men. For example, a well-planned kickoff event in the fall can give your ministry a good jumpstart. This kind of event provides opportunity to share with the men of your church what the men's ministry is going to be doing in the months ahead and how they can be involved. Many see the fall as a new beginning, and they may be more inclined to join a small group that's just starting. One year every man who came to our fall kickoff received a copy of *Man in the Mirror* by Pat Morley and a schedule of all the new small groups that were going to study the book. Many men who'd never been in a small group joined one. Again, it's not that events and activities are bad—use them to enhance your ministry to men instead of just keeping men busy.

■ Based on Random Activities

After a leader rattles off his grocery list of events, I'll ask how the retreat relates to the Saturday breakfast and how the breakfast ties to the small groups and how the small groups connect to the service project. This usually elicits a long stare! The leader usually asks, "What do you mean?" So I repeat the question. Most of the time, no relationship exists between the various aspects of the ministry.

The solution is to move toward designing men's ministry with a purpose. Everything you do should have a purpose. The various activities need to be interrelated. Later we'll look at how you can develop a purpose statement for your ministry.

■ Based on Methods

Most of us are enamored with success. If something's working for someone else, I'll pick up that model and try it. This happens in churches and their ministries too. It also happens in the men's ministry arena. Often when I ask leaders why they're taking a certain approach in their men's ministry, they tell me it's because they read about a church across the city—or even the country—with a successful ministry using that approach.

Instead of being drawn to better methods and strategies, we need to explore and apply biblical principles explicitly stated in Scripture. The Bible doesn't explain just the message we're to share with men. It also gives us a philosophy and principles for doing ministry. Each church is unique, with a unique history, culture, personality, and philosophy of ministry. It's safe to say that each church's men's ministry will be unique, as well. God wants to develop a ministry unique to your church and community that will most effectively minister to the men within and outside of your church.

Obviously, this isn't an exhaustive list of the problems men's ministries face. But I hope it will help you avoid some of the more common mistakes as you start or grow your church's ministry to men.

Why Every Church Needs a Thriving Ministry to Men

The fact that you're reading this may mean that I'm "preaching to the choir" here. But let me state the obvious. There are at least six good reasons why every church needs a specific ministry to men.

■ The American Male Is in Great Need

Men today are in crisis. They're confused over what it means and doesn't mean to be a man. Every ten years, the model changes. For a while it was the John Wayne "tough guy." Then it was the James Bond "womanizer." Then the Phil Donohue "sensitive male." Then the Michael Douglas "Wall Street climber."

On top of that, the American male is friendless. The average man over thirty-five doesn't have one close friend he can call in the middle of the night.

The American male is sexually addicted. With the Internet making this addiction private, men spend more and more time in front of the computer staring at touched-up images of "perfect" women. And Christian men haven't escaped this addiction.

The American male is emotionally isolated. When asked what he's feeling, the average guy will say either "good" or "bad." The problem is, neither of these is a feeling. Men struggle with identifying and expressing their emotions in a healthy manner. Most funnel every emotion through anger. So whether they're sad, scared, frustrated, fearful, or joyful, they still kick the cat when they get home.

The American male is searching spiritually. In the midst of this gloomy picture of men, one thing is true: They're looking for something beyond themselves to make sense out of the world they live in and the problems they face. For this reason, men need a place they can go to deal with these issues. They desire a place of safety and refuge where they can be who they are and accepted as they are. In his book *Everybody's Normal Till You Get to Know Them*, John Ortberg says that we're all born with a tag on us that reads, "As Is."

Within the context of a small group for men, someone struggling with these needs will have the opportunity to share his struggles, hurts, concerns, dreams, and victories. The other men in his group can stand with him, encouraging, cheering, comforting, and supporting him as they walk through life together. Of course, it doesn't always work this way in churches today. We end up judging each other and acting phony, trying to give the impression that we're good

Christian men. But when men in small groups start to relate to each other the way God intended—experiencing trust, authenticity, and honesty—they'll feel free to share who they are and what's going on in their lives.

■ Men Will Come to Know Jesus

Men today vote with their feet and by their absence. For most men, the traditional way of doing church doesn't work. When a man walks into church, he has to become everything he is not.

We'll reach men for Christ not by having them come to our churches but rather by the church going to them. One study of four hundred unchurched executives who worked in downtown Chicago asked: "If you were to talk to someone about spiritual things, who would you talk to? (1) a pastor/priest, (2) an evangelist, (3) a family member or relative, or (4) the person right next to you." It shouldn't surprise us that 80 percent said they'd talk with the man or woman working in the cubicle or office next to them—someone going through the same struggles they are.

Every study says the same thing: Most people come to Christ through a relationship with a friend or relative. If we desire to bring men to Christ, it will likely happen in the context of life with men of the church building long-term relationships of integrity with men in the world.

■ Men Will Grow Into Followers of Jesus

Unfortunately, too many baby Christian men are running around our churches today. They may have attended church for thirty years, but they're still babies. Like Peter Pan, they seem to be saying, "I don't want to grow up!"

A men's ministry can be a place where men are intentionally discipled. Through small groups, mentoring, and in other relationships with spiritually growing men, guys learn the basics of walking with Jesus.

■ Men Will Move Out of the Pews

Every man in your church has gifts that would allow him to serve in the church. But many men approach church as they do the NFL—they're couch potatoes. Christianity isn't a spectator sport; there's no place for bench sitting in the church.

An effective men's ministry can help men discover their gifts and spark their passion and interest to plug into ministry.

■ Men Will Build Authentic Relationships

Christianity isn't a solo sport either. It's a team sport. Most men are naturally drawn toward isolation and independence. But Scripture is clear that from the very beginning of time we were made by God for community.

Again, a small group can be a place where the men of your church learn what it means to enter into authentic and encouraging relationships with other men. They can find comfort when they walk through difficult times and be held accountable as they work to chip away character flaws in their lives. Building these types of relationships can only happen in the context of a few men meeting together week after week.

■ Men Will Become Leaders

Our culture has a dearth of leadership. No matter what aspect of society you look at—the home, government, education, business, athletics, or the church—you'll see a shortage of leaders. There's a crying need for leadership. Leaders aren't born; they're made.

A men's ministry can help a man shape his character, refine his skills, develop his worldview, and ignite his passion to stand up and lead in the arenas God places him.

When I look at the potential of what can happen when we take seriously the call to minister to men in the church, I get excited. The sleeping giant could be awakened; revival could be right around the corner. For the past ten years, I've seen this happening at our church. Hundreds of men are becoming the men God intends them to be. They're coming to Christ, growing up in Christ, serving Christ all over the church, building relationships, and willingly taking the mantle of leadership. I know this can happen in your church as well.

Now that we have a vision of what men's ministry in your church could accomplish, I'd like to take you to 35,000 feet for a different perspective. I want to help you understand the importance of developing a purpose and philosophy of ministry before you jump into the how to's of doing ministry. We often start doing things without a proper biblical base or without knowing why we're doing what we're doing. But don't get frustrated and think you have to accomplish all of this at once. Instead, be encouraged by what your ministry could look like five or six years from now.

Doing Ministry With a Purpose

Jesus was a man of purpose—he knew where he came from, why

he came, and where he was going. This awareness affected everything: where he went, who he hung around with, and what he did. His purpose for living affected everything about his life.

If you want to minister to and with men, you need to be aware of your purpose. It affects everything you do. Jesus said, "Go and make disciples of all nations, baptizing them in the name of the Father and of the Son and of the Holy Spirit, and teaching them to obey everything I have commanded you. And surely I am with you always, to the very end of the age" (Matthew 28:19-20). In addition to being a command to his followers, this statement sums up the single mission of Jesus' own life. The command is to "make disciples." A disciple is a follower, learner, and imitator. Jesus doesn't instruct us to make converts or good church attendees, but to make disciples. How to do that is found in these three phrases:

1. Go. This might be better translated "as you go." As you go through life, make disciples. Disciple-making takes place in the everyday activity of life—as you go to work, to the fitness center, to the ballgame, and home. Going is about relationships.

2. Baptize. This means to identify with the cause of Christ—both his person and work. Baptism is an external expression of an inner reality. Baptism shows a commitment to follow Christ.

3. Teach. This verb speaks of helping disciples grow into mature followers of Jesus. It also represents how they can build their own disciple-making ministries as well.

So what's the overriding purpose of our ministry to men? To make disciples, who will make disciples, who will make disciples.

Ken Adams, author of *Becoming an Authentic Disciple,* says, "God's goal for the church was simply to be an environment for making disciples. The church should be nothing more than a group of people who are being and building disciples by calling people to come and see, follow, remain and go out in Jesus' name. God wants the church to have the mission of Jesus."

The purpose of having a ministry to men is much greater than just helping men be better husbands, fathers, and workers. These are good things but not the best. The goal of a men's ministry is to reach people who don't know Jesus. The only way to accomplish this goal is through men who seriously take Christ's command to make disciples.

Developing a Philosophy of Ministry

Reaching this goal requires a clearly defined philosophy of ministry. Once again, Jesus provides the best model for developing a philosophy of ministry. Jesus was the first man to do men's ministry, and we can learn a lot from him.

Let's look at five different areas of Jesus' life as we develop our philosophy of ministry.

1. Pray

Your ministry to men will only move forward on its knees. Prayer wasn't a part of Jesus' life—it was his life. He prayed in private and in public, in crises, and in the everyday aspects of life. Prayer was such a significant part of his life that when the disciples came upon him praying, they asked him to teach them how to pray. Even the slow-learning disciples recognized that the uniqueness and strength of Christ's life were based on his walk with his heavenly Father in prayer. It needs to pervade our lives as well. Here are a few verses that exemplify his prayer life:

- "But Jesus often withdrew to lonely places and prayed" (Luke 5:16).

- "One of those days Jesus went out to a mountainside to pray, and spent the night praying to God" (Luke 6:12).

- "One day Jesus was praying in a certain place. When he finished, one of his disciples said to him, 'Lord, teach us to pray, just as John taught his disciples' " (Luke 11:1).

A ministry to men will start with a commitment to prayer by you and others with a passion to reach the men of your church and community. As Robert Murray McCheyne said, "A prayerful man is a fearful weapon in the hands of a Holy God." Withdraw on a daily basis to a quiet place to do kingdom business with God—a place where you can put the hearts of the men of your church into the hands of God. Enlist others to pray. If you desire to have an effective ministry to men, it must begin and end with prayer.

2. Evangelize

When you study the life of Jesus, you quickly realize that the hearts of people were of utmost importance to him. The New Testament contains more than fifty accounts of Jesus spending time with people in need of a Savior. In Matthew 9:9-13, Jesus called Matthew, the tax collector; in Luke 19:1-10, he invited himself to have dinner with Zacchaeus; in John 4:4-26, Jesus interacted with the woman at the well; in Mark 2:15-17, Jesus interacted with tax collectors and others who society looked down on.

Jesus modeled the priority of helping people enter a relationship with him. After he called the initial disciples to himself, he exhorted them to become "fishers of men." To find balance in your ministry to men, keep this principle in mind to focus on this priority.

People matter to God. People are lost and in desperate need of the Savior. In his book *Victorious Christian Service*, Alan Redpath says, "You never lighten the load unless first you have felt the pressure in your own soul. You are never used of God to bring blessing until God has opened your eyes and made you see things as they are." Until we believe in the core of our being that people will spend eternity separated from God, we'll have little impact in people's lives.

Evangelism is relationship building. Evangelism is a process with many steps. Jesus used the analogy of farming to convey this process. A farmer doesn't plant seed one day and harvest the next. Instead, he tills the ground and prepares it for planting. Then he must weed it, water it, fertilize it, and allow the sun to shine on it. Only after months and months of hard work are the fields ready for harvest. The same is true in the lives of men. Evangelism is the process of helping men take baby steps closer and closer to the Cross. When you help them see Jesus more clearly and help them get rid of false caricatures about Christianity, you're involved in evangelism.

Supplement personal evangelistic efforts. This may mean planning a quality event designed to reach non-Christian men. This isn't a time for fellowship, in-depth Bible teaching, or extended worship. It may take time for the men of your church to catch the vision for what you're trying to do. Encourage the men of your church to attend only if they bring guests who don't have a relationship with Jesus.

3. Establish

Almost half of Jesus' ministry was spent developing relationships with men who later became leaders of the church. His goal was to assist men in getting rooted, established, and built up in the faith. He desired men to have a solid knowledge of himself and know what it was to trust, obey, follow, and walk with him the rest of their lives. Jesus taught the disciples these basic kingdom values in the Sermon on the Mount (Matthew 5–7). He spoke of the character, piety, priorities, influence, and love of those who follow him.

When it comes to working with men, keep these principles in mind.

Preaching builds the church; discipleship builds men. The easy part of ministry is drawing a crowd. The hard part is building that crowd into devoted followers of Jesus. Churches are full of a lot of baby Christians who need to grow up and learn to walk with Jesus on their own. This doesn't just happen. A disciple-making ministry requires an increasing number of disciple makers—men who'll walk with these babies week after week, month after month.

Spiritual formation happens in a variety of ways. But you'll help men grow if you concentrate on these three areas.

- Help men establish spiritual disciplines in their lives. This will give them experience with a deeper communion with God.

- Help them realize that Christianity isn't a solo sport. Growing means surrounding themselves with other men who will be their Paul, Timothy, and Barnabas. A "Paul" is someone more mature than you, who acts as a mentor or coach in various aspects of your life. A "Timothy" is someone less mature in the faith than you—someone you build your life into, helping to get started in the faith or to grow up into Christlikeness. A "Barnabas" is a peer who can speak the truth, encourage, and comfort you when you walk through the valleys of life.

- Help them learn to serve to enhance their spiritual growth. Encourage your men to share their faith, find their place of service in the church, take part in corporate worship, and give to the local church.

Small groups are where relationships and spiritual growth happen. In the context of relationships—where men can find support, encouragement, accountability, and prayer—character can be shaped, skills honed, and worldview enlarged. The small group is the optimal place for spiritual growth to take place.

In all aspects of your ministry, uphold the centrality of God's Word. There's little doubt of how important the Word of God was to Jesus. More than ninety times he referred to the Old Testament, quoting from more than seventy chapters. The Bible is God's manual for living and ministering. Get men into the Word, and you'll see their lives change.

4. Equip

The goal of this area of ministry is identifying and equipping men to serve in the local church. You'll be raising up an army of men to fulfill the Great Commission among their peers. Once again, Jesus provides the example. In an intentional way, Jesus prepared his followers for service in the kingdom. In Mark 6:7-11, Jesus sent out the Twelve to minister; in Luke 10:1-16, he sends an expanded team out to minister. Throughout his ministry, Jesus constantly gave his disciples the opportunity to be stretched and used in kingdom expansion and extension. Keep the following principles in mind regarding this phase of ministry.

You must be convinced regarding the priesthood of all believers. All men are gifted to serve Christ. I regularly tell the men of our church, "Every man is a starter." What I mean is that in God's economy, there's no such thing as bench-sitters or second-stringers. Every man has a role to play in God's redemptive plans. Your job as a leader is to get men out of the stands and into the game—out of the pews and onto the streets for Christ.

Workers are built in relationships. You can't develop workers for Christ in a classroom. Instead, as mature believers interact and spend time with men, they see firsthand what it's like to use their spiritual gifts for the cause of Christ. Put them in a variety of experiences that allow them to discover their gifts. The best way men can discover their gifts is to just do it.

Bud Wilkinson was one of the greatest college football coaches ever. Shortly after retiring from the University of Oklahoma, he was asked to head up the President's Council on Physical Fitness. At the opening press conference, a reporter asked Wilkinson why football was so good for the country. Wilkinson responded that football was actually bad for the country. When the stunned reporter asked why football was bad, Wilkinson answered, "Football is eighty thousand people desperately in need of exercise watching twenty-two men desperately in need of rest…We need to get those twenty-two men in need of rest on the sideline, and get the eighty thousand people in the stands onto the field." What a description of the church today! As leaders, our job is to get the men of our churches out of the pews and into the game.

5. Empower

When you empower others, you start developing leaders who can carry on the ministry after you move on. Jesus knew he had only three years to develop the disciples into men who'd continue the work after he was gone. They were alongside him in ministry experiences and were ready for leadership responsibilities after Jesus' resurrection. In John 13–17 we get a taste of specific training and instruction that empowered the disciples for establishing the early church.

Developing leaders is the most important thing you can do. It's perhaps the most important lasting investment you can make as a leader. Willow Creek Pastor Bill Hybels said, "Leaders are at their best when they are raising up other leaders. They are looking for emerging leaders, investing in them and empowering them for the work of the kingdom. They leave a legacy of leadership."[1]

Keep in mind the "Leadership Pipeline." The leadership process requires an intentional plan and hard work. The leadership pipeline means you keep the end in mind when developing your leadership training process. As a leadership team, you'll need to decide what qualities you want to build into your men. Developing leaders includes the following:

- character formation—the being
- competency development—the doing
- cognitive training—the knowing
- calling clarification—the focus
- chemistry—leading as a team
- communion—in relationship to God and one another

Coaching them. Emerging leaders need proximity to the real deal. You coach by providing encouragement, direction, evaluation, and prayer. This means setting up individual meetings with your leaders to talk about how they're doing, what they're learning, where they want prayer, and how you can resource them to better do their ministry.

To read more about developing leaders and putting together a leadership team for your men's ministry, see "Leadership Team: Winning the Battle to Find Great Leaders" starting on page 34.

Make the Philosophy Practical

OK, you've already accomplished a lot! You've explored what men's ministry is and, just as importantly, what it isn't. You've looked at some of the common problems with men's ministry and given some thought about how to avoid making those mistakes in your church's ministry to men. You've examined both the cultural and personal reasons why your church needs a thriving men's ministry. And you've studied how Jesus provided the perfect model for developing a philosophy of ministry to men.

However, all the action so far seems to be taking place above the neckline—only in your mind and, if you're fortunate, in the minds of some like-minded potential leaders. Maybe you're afraid to take the next step. Or maybe you're ready to start your men's ministry today! No matter what you're feeling, let's look at some practical ways you can put some arms and legs on your church's emerging ministry to men.

Gather Pastoral Support

One preliminary but very practical step you can take early on is soliciting the support of your senior pastor. Without his or her support, you'll find it very difficult to proceed with your ministry to men. Your pastor may get excited because others are grabbing hold of ministry and running. Pastors also can be nervous because they don't know where a ministry is headed—and often they end up doing the ministry if those who start it leave. They also have the advantage of seeing the big picture of the entire church and what other demands they'll face if a new ministry begins. Here are a few steps to get your pastor's involvement and support.

Include your pastor. Early on, meet with your pastor to talk about your passion and vision for starting a ministry to men. Ask what plans he or she has for the men of the church. Your pastor may just be waiting for someone to step up to the plate to help. On the other hand, your pastor and church leaders may have other new ministries planned for the upcoming year. If you're asked to wait a year, it wouldn't be a bad thing. You can still do a number of things. First, ask how you and your team can help accomplish the broader mission of the church in the coming year. Your pastor may have a larger vision, such as buying property for a new building or planting a daughter church. Perhaps your team can pray for that on a regular basis. Or you can start developing your leadership team and begin the process of getting to know each other and growing deeper in the Lord. Don't see it as a wasted year—but as one that will lay the foundation for the future.

Inform your pastor. Ask your pastor how much he or she wants to be included in developing the new ministry. Your pastor may want to attend the retreat when you develop a purpose statement and put together an initial strategy. Your pastor may want to attend your monthly planning meetings, hear a report following your meetings, or just get together once a year to talk about how things are going. Bottom line, ask your pastor at what level he or she wants to be involved and informed.

Intercede for your pastor. There's no greater gift you can give your pastor than to pray on a regular basis. If you have an initial leadership team in place, ask how the team can pray for your pastor and the church each week. Split up the week, with a different leader on your team committing to pray the same day each week.

Encourage your pastor. There's no more difficult job in the world than being a pastor. Pastors serve as CEOs, providing vision, direction, and motivation for the church. On the other hand, pastors serve as shepherds and servants, caring for the souls of the church. Write your pastor notes, make calls, and express your appreciation for his or her ministry.

Develop a Purpose Statement

When you ask most men's ministry leaders, "What's the purpose for your ministry?" chances are their first response will be a blank stare. Many ministries fail because of a lack of purpose, direction, and focus. A clear and concise purpose statement will give your ministry direction, keep your team focused, help you evaluate your ministry, and inspire everyone to move forward. A purpose statement is a concise written expression that captures your current thinking about why your church's men's ministry should exist. Your purpose statement will guide implementing a strategy for ministry to and with men in your church. Another way to say it is, What role does God want our ministry to play in his greater purpose of the Great Commission?

Look at these examples of purpose statements:

- "To help men be disciples and to make disciples."

- "To empower men to know Christ and to make him known."

- "To equip men for personal holiness and global impact."

- "To empower men to build authentic relationships with Jesus Christ and, inspired by the Holy Spirit, become godly influences in their world."

Guidelines for writing a purpose statement. Putting together your purpose statement won't happen overnight; it's a team effort that might take several months. There are a couple of ways you can approach the process:

- Schedule three consecutive meetings. For example, schedule three Monday nights in a row to work on it as a team. Give various men homework to complete so that when you meet, much of the background work is already done.

- Schedule a weekend retreat. If you spent Friday evening and most of the day Saturday working on it, you'd be able to get it finished.

Some basic steps for writing your purpose statement:

- Do a study of the biblical passages that speak to God's purposes for Christ-followers and the church. For example, read and talk about Matthew 28:19-20; Ephesians 4:11-12; Colossians 1:28; Colossians 2:6-7; and 2 Timothy 2:2. Have team members study these and other passages on their own while asking the question, What do these say about ministry to men?

- When you come together, talk about the findings of the team. What major themes run through these passages? What are those themes you sense God calling your ministry to? Some of the key words you come up with might include teaching, compassion, discipling, and evangelism.

- Do an evaluation of your church's purpose statement. Break down your church's statement to see what purposes the whole church desires to accomplish. You want to be sure that your ministry supplements what the church is doing and doesn't veer off in a different direction.

- Begin writing your purpose statement. Your team will have to answer the following questions: Why does this ministry exist? How can we supplement what the whole church is doing? What does God want us to be as a ministry? What are we to be doing as a ministry? What are some action words we can use to communicate the purpose?

- Develop a rough draft. Spend time as a team crafting a one- or two-sentence statement that expresses why you exist as a ministry. Then pray about it and give yourselves some time to ponder it. As a team, return to it a few weeks later and make revisions.

Evaluate your purpose statement. When you land on a statement you all agree to, ask yourselves the following questions: Is it clear and concise? Is it easy to communicate to the leaders and men of the church? Is it consistent with who we are as a church? Does it empower the leaders of the ministry?

Communicate your statement to the church. One of the toughest jobs you'll face is communicating your purpose to the men in your church. But if you go through the trouble of crafting this statement, and you truly believe God desires you to move forward, you'll want to make sure the men of your church know what you're about and how they can get on board. This means you have to communicate, communicate, communicate. Let's look at a few ideas to get you started.

- Communicate it personally. When Jimmy Carter talks about Habitat for Humanity, he's not in a three-piece suit. Instead, he's in his work clothes on a roof pounding nails. Jimmy Carter embodies what Habitat is. The most effective way you can communicate the purpose of your men's ministry is to "live it" as a ministry team. If your purpose is outreach, your leaders should all be sharing their faith with others. If your purpose is discipling, then you should all be building into the lives of others.

- Communicate one on one. Take the opportunity to share your ministry's purpose whenever you get together with other men of the church. Explain it to them and help them see where they might fit into it.

- Communicate it publicly. Through a testimony during church services or when speaking at any large group that includes the men of the church, express concisely why your men's ministry exists.

- Communicate it through print. When you send out fliers, registration forms, or brochures, make sure you include why the ministry exists and how the event or activity you're promoting fits into the overall strategy of the ministry.

- Communicate through the Web. Ask your pastor if you can get a place on the church's Web site to describe the men's ministry. You'll need someone who can keep the information up to date, but it's well worth the effort.

Build a Prayer Team

In the church today, we seem to spend a great deal of time talking about prayer, singing about prayer, and reading about prayer. But we don't spend that much time in prayer. Here are a couple of principles for building a prayer team:

Find a group of men who'll pray for your ministry team. Ask men to commit to pray for the men's ministry once each week. They can decide when and where they'll pray. It's encouraging to know that men are praying throughout the week for you and the budding activities of the ministry.

Send requests to the team. Once you have a prayer team, be sure you keep them updated on requests and answers to prayer as God works. Nothing is more encouraging to a prayer life than to see God's answers.

Move Forward and Grow

Everything we've discussed to this point can easily take a year or more for you and your leadership team to accomplish. This is normal and helpful, as you'll have a great foundation for many years of fruitful ministry. As you move ahead from this point, keep some basic principles in mind as you think through your program and what it's going to look like.

Go slow. Ministry isn't a hundred-yard dash. It's more of a marathon. Think in terms of four to five years of slowly building your ministry. If you move too quickly without a good foundation, the whole ministry can collapse with a single hiccup. For a basic outline of what those first few years might look like, see Toolbox page 33.

Start small. Remember, numbers aren't important. If Jesus had been judged by numbers, he'd have been considered a failure. Of course, we know that his plan works and that numbers aren't the measure for judging whether ministry is successful or not. Stick to Jesus' plan—work with a small group of men who'll in turn work with others. Take this group of leaders and teach them what it means to fall in love with Jesus and to invest their lives in others.

See ministry as a process. Ministry to men isn't an isolated event. It's an intentional series of steps to help men move toward being fully devoted followers of Jesus. Men will enter the ministry at different times and at different places in their faith journeys. Instead of seeing this as a problem, see it as an opportunity to minister to more men. Keep these basic concepts in mind as you view the process of ministry:

- Start where men are and move them toward where they need to go. Some men will come into your ministry without any previous connection to church or God. Others may come as new Christians. Some will be men who've been around the church most of their lives. Others will be leaders-in-the-making. Still others may be very mature and motivated leaders. Wherever they're starting from, take them from that point and slowly move them forward. Challenge them not to settle for where they are; always set the bar a little higher.

- Build bridges to the next level of maturity. As you begin to put together various programs, keep in mind that everything should have a purpose and fit into the bigger picture. For example, if you decide to have a Saturday breakfast, offer those who attend the opportunity to join small groups. Your small groups might be entry-level groups with just a six-week commitment. At the end of that time, ask the men if they want to continue for another ten weeks. At each step of the way, raise the commitment level just a little.

- Provide a variety of open doors. One question you want to ask your leaders is, What open doors is God giving us for ministry right now? For example, the topic of fathering is popular in our culture right now. Most dads both in the church and outside the church are interested in being better fathers. Offer a Saturday seminar with a guest speaker and some break-out small groups for discussion afterward. Other key subjects for men currently are work, finances, sports, and spirituality.

- Decentralize your men's ministry. The best ministry happens where men feel most comfortable. That's not the church; it's the marketplace. You may find it most effective to have your men's small groups meet in the workplace. These groups will provide opportunities for guys to meet with a few other men whom they can slowly get to know.

Keep the Ministry Personal

I'd like to close by going back to the beginning. Remember what men's ministry is? It's "one man walking with another man, helping him to know Christ in a deeper way." It's about people. It's about building relationships. Men's ministry is about guys working with other guys to bring glory to God, and through their relationships growing closer to Jesus.

After all this talk of problems, principles, purpose statements, and programs, it's easy to feel overwhelmed and discouraged. Just remember that in the kingdom of God, the closer you get to people, the greater the impact you'll have in their lives. To put it another way, the effectiveness of your ministry will be directly related to the relationships that you develop and maintain.

In 1 Thessalonians 2:8-9, Paul says: "We loved you so much that we were delighted to share with you not only the gospel of God but our lives as well, because you had become so dear to us. Surely you remember, brothers, our toil and hardship; we worked night and day in order not to be a burden to anyone while we preached the gospel of God to you."

Paul is saying that he wasn't interested in riding into the city on a big white horse, dropping some sermon bombs on people, and then leaving. While he enjoyed preaching the gospel, what really got him fired up was sharing his life with others. He valued his relationships above everything else.

Later Paul notes that he'd been like both a mother and father to the Thessalonian church. As a mother, he cared for them—like a mother with a nursing baby imparting nourishment and life to her young child. As a father he encouraged, comforted, and urged them to live lives worthy of the Lord—almost like a caring coach who trains and encourages his players to be all that they can be.

As you spend time with the men of your church, always keep relationship in mind. Listen to them, pray for them, walk with them, love them, and encourage them in their faith.

That's what men's ministry is.

Steve Sonderman

As one of only a handful of full-time men's pastors in the United States, Steve Sonderman is on the leading edge of local church ministry to men. Steve has been an associate pastor at Elmbrook Church in Brookfield, Wisconsin, for the past eighteen years. His passion to see every local church have its own ministry to men has led him to begin Top Gun Ministries. Steve and his wife, Colleen, have four children.

Visit his Web site at: www.topgunministries.org.

Endnotes

1. Bill Hybels, "Developing Emerging Leaders," quoted at the Leadership Summit, Willow Creek Church, August 1999.

CHAPTER 1 TOOLBOX

Men's Ministry Start-Up Timeline

■ Year 1

Assemble your leadership team and spend the year becoming for one another what you want the men of your church to be. During this year, you'll do a lot of preparation work: developing your prayer team, surveying the men of the church, writing a purpose statement, and getting your pastor's input and support.

■ Year 2

Begin to develop an identity within the church. You want the men of the church to know a ministry to men exists. You might add to your leadership team and kick off one area of ministry such as a Saturday breakfast, small groups, or quarterly seminars.

■ Year 3

Spread your wings. Look for open doors for your ministry and go through them. Pick one new area of ministry and do it. Aim for one new area of ministry a year. Before beginning a new aspect of ministry, have a leader who's willing to be the point person. This leader should develop a team of people to work with him and a purpose statement and strategy for the new aspect of ministry. (This all sounds familiar, doesn't it?) During this year, your overall men's ministry will continue to provide training for existing leaders and new leaders for the ministry.

■ Year 4

Continue to move forward and fill in empty spots. With your leadership team, evaluate where your ministry is unbalanced and make plans for finding balance. Evaluate if your leadership team is functioning properly or if it needs to be realigned with how the ministry has grown. Because some of the men on your leadership team may move or decide to switch ministries within the church, ask each leader to work with an apprentice. When you meet with them individually, ask the leader who he is preparing to take his position if he moves on. By doing this, you're preparing new leaders if men leave or if your ministry grows.

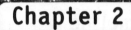

Chapter 2

LEADERSHIP TEAM: WINNING THE BATTLE TO FIND GREAT LEADERS

Greg, Phil, and Mark sat around a small table at the coffee shop.

"A double espresso? What's the deal, Greg? Rough night?"

"I was up all night on the phone with a friend from church. He's leaving his wife for some woman at work."

"Is he a Christian?"

"Yeah, but he doesn't really see this conflicting with his faith. He actually said to me, 'God wants me to be happy and I'm not. I'll still be there for the kids. Actually it's better for them! They can live in two happy homes instead of one miserable one.' "

"How can we be so deceived? There's a guy at church dealing with an addiction to pornography. He's convinced he can compartmentalize his 'problem' without it affecting the rest of his life."

"Don't forget Rob—he doesn't even have a 'rest of his life' because he spends all his time at the office."

"Why can't we speak into these guys lives? Why can't we intervene before the destruction?"

"Hey, man! We're not an army—we're just three guys with our own coffee addiction!"

As Greg, Phil, and Mark continued talking, they wondered if the army idea might be an appropriate one after all. If only they had a special force that could move in and influence a few men who could then influence a few more men...

Sounds like the start of a leadership team for a men's ministry.

Building a Team of Leaders

In order to begin an identifiable ministry to men in your church or to take your existing men's ministry to the next level of effectiveness, you need to assemble a team of dedicated people to organize and lead the effort.

It helps to use terminology that men can relate to. You'll need to determine the best way to communicate your approach to ministry with the terminology and models that already exist in your church. For example, one church may talk in terms of football or other team sports, while another church may use outdoor adventure themes. Whatever you choose, it should appeal to men and make sense within the culture of your local community.

As we explore putting together a leadership team here, we'll use military terms to describe the key components and processes. While some guys might not naturally be drawn to these descriptions, building a men's leadership team is a lot like assembling an army. And since a great spiritual battle is already taking place—the forces of darkness against God's kingdom—it's appropriate to think of men's ministry as a battle for the souls of men.

Most men are attracted to causes with clear purposes and credible people involved. Some men may get involved in your men's ministry because of a particular event or program, but they'll only stay if they enjoy being around the men who are there. "As iron sharpens iron, so one man sharpens another" (Proverbs 27:17). This applies to your leaders as well—what each leader models will help shape what the men of your church will become. So it pays to choose your leaders wisely.

Twelve Steps to Developing Your Team

Obviously, before your men's ministry has anything to offer, someone needs to step up to lead. Over time, you'll need more than a "someone" to lead. You'll require a whole team of leaders if you want to accomplish effective ministry. Put in our army terms, you'll need to marshal generals, commanders, and other officers before you can enlist the rest of the troops.

Reaching men through other men using groups and teams is God's idea. Jesus had twelve disciples. David had his mighty men. The early church had overseers and deacons. Similarly you need an organized force to reach men—a band of volunteers who pledge allegiance to Christ and vow to rally alongside your church.

The following diagram provides a snapshot of what developing a team might look like.

PHASES	STAGES
Phase 1: Prepare	*Identify Objectives—Personal Passion* 1. Call to Arms 2. Assemble Command Unit 3. Capture the Vision (Report Initial Intelligence) *Coordinate with HQ—Your Church's Blessing* 4. Receive Orders (Cast the Vision) 5. Formulate a Battle Plan 6. Set Up Base of Operations
Phase 2: Mobilize	*Strengthen Your Force—Your Leaders* 7. Recruit 8. Train 9. Deploy *Adapt on the Battle Field—Always Improve* 10. Assess Progress 11. Enhance Tactics 12. Hone Tools

As you can see, putting together an ideal leadership team happens in two main phases: prepare and mobilize. Each phase has a series of stages. It all looks so good on paper, doesn't it? But you're working with people, not paper! As you develop your team, you'll likely move through these stages. But the order of the process will depend on the culture and people in your church.

So think of this as a battle plan for finding great leaders for your men's ministry. But also think of the plan as one that can change and adapt. Be open to change and sensitive to the unique character and personality of your team. Ask God to reveal to you where to start and what the greatest needs are. Think of it as a journey, an adventure, an investment. Set your sights on learning and enjoying the process rather than achieving some ideal outcome. Let God take care of the outcome.

Let's take a closer look at the battle plan—particularly the twelve phases and what they involve.

1. Call to Arms

Like Greg, Phil, and Mark talking at the coffee shop, maybe you're tired of seeing guys fall by the wayside instead of thriving in their God-given roles as men, husbands, and fathers. It grieves you to see the issues that the men of your church are dealing with. And you're even a bit angry that the Enemy seems to be successfully picking off the men of faith around you.

The good news is that God is moving in the hearts of men. He's calling men to stand up for what they believe in—to serve in his army of the faithful. That's the first step in developing your leaders—recognizing the passion that's been awakened in your midst.

This is a divine *call to arms!* God has a plan for accomplishing his objectives and neutralizing the Enemy's threats. Seek God and listen to him. Psalm 127:1 says, "Unless the Lord builds the house, its builders labor in vain. Unless the Lord watches over the city, the watchmen stand guard in vain."

Asking others to follow God's call to arms is an awesome responsibility. Take the time to search your own heart and be convinced of your own commitment to leading men before inviting other leaders to join you.

2. Assemble Command Unit

The Old Testament is full of stories of great warriors called by God. But none of them were individual snipers. They all drew a select group of leaders around them. In your men's ministry, you also need to build an intimate command unit around you.

Your basic command unit will be made up of the following people:

- commander
- staff sponsor/ally
- one or two wise advisers

Ministry commander. This is the person who puts time and energy into making things happen within men's ministry. He's not the only person called to lead, and he's not solely responsible for making things happen. But he's the guy who gets things rolling. He puts together and maintains your command unit.

Do you have a commander now? Is God leading you or someone else to step forward to be the commander? Your commander should be able to answer the following questions with a resounding "yes!"

- Are you committed to living as a man of God? Have you allowed God to work in your life to build into you the qualities, gifts, and places of service he desires for you?
- Does your heart long to see other men in your church walk closely with Christ?
- Does the thought of leading a team of men to reach other men energize you?

Ministry sponsor/ally. The second person in the command unit is a primary ally within the ranks of the church staff—the senior pastor, an associate pastor, a staff director, or in a smaller church, perhaps an elder or deacon. The sponsor is your headquarters liaison, the church leader who is committed to helping men's ministry succeed. He (or she) must have sufficient influence with key decision makers to help the men's ministry accomplish its goals. The ministry sponsor doesn't necessarily devote extra time to men's ministry, but supports and promotes things up the chain of command when needed.

Adviser(s). Finally, you'll want to add one or two more men to the command unit—or even more, depending on the size of your church. Look for men passionate about the prospects of men's ministry. They also need to be men with time—the next few steps will require both hard work and wise counsel.

3. Capture the Vision

Perhaps you're embarking on this adventure because you have a senior pastor who's passionate about men's ministry (or maybe you are that wise pastor). You're like a commissioned officer who's been given the charge to "make it so!" If this describes you, you can probably fold this step into "Formulate a Battle Plan" because you already have the blessing and encouragement of your church's leaders.

But if you're on more of a stealth mission to bless your church in ways no one has even dreamed about, you have some selling to do. Start by drawing a broad-stroke vision statement. This isn't a detailed battle plan; it's more like an initial intelligence report that you'll take to your church leadership. This vision statement can also motivate other leaders to join you when they learn what you're trying to accomplish.

Here's an example of a broad vision statement: We purpose together to lead men into authentic Christ-centered relationships with significance for today and a lasting legacy for tomorrow.

As you put together a vision statement for your men's ministry, you want to be specific enough so that others capture a sense of where you're going. Yet you want to be loose enough with details so that you can easily incorporate creative new ideas as new leaders join your team. The following questions can help you create a vision statement:

- What's our main purpose for starting a men's ministry? What's our core mission, vision, or approach for reaching men?

- Who do we want to reach—who are our target constituents? Is the primary audience the men in our church and community—and by extension, the families in our church and community?

- What methods do we think we'll use? What's our philosophy of ministry?

- Do we have a basic structure (the command unit or leadership team) in place?

- Do we have ideas about what activities and programs we might incorporate into our ministry? Have we thought through how those elements link together?

- Do we have a basic idea of how we'll pay our own way or how the larger church will support us?

- If asked, what recommendations would we make to the church leadership about proceeding with a ministry to men?

Obviously the answers to all of these questions won't be part of your vision statement. But by being armed with this intelligence report, you're ready to approach your church leadership.

4. Receive Orders

As you establish your leadership team, commit at the outset to conduct your men's ministry activities under the authority of, within the boundaries set by, and with the blessing of your local church. That means you'll need to clearly communicate what you're doing with the top decision makers of your church. The more church leaders you can communicate your vision to, the more support your ministry will enjoy. List key individuals and groups within your church that you want to communicate with:

- elders, deacons, council (or whatever your church calls its main governing body)

- senior pastor

- paid pastoral/ministry staff members

- lay ministry directors or leaders

Set up times to present your vision for men's ministry to various individuals and groups that make up the leadership in your church. Pray about what you're going to say. As you put together a presentation of your proposal, consider including the following:

- Cast the vision—What's the main goal you'll accomplish through this ministry?

- State the purpose—Why do you want to start this ministry?

- Emphasize the tie to the overall church vision—How is this men's ministry vital to the health and growth of your church?

- Alleviate objections—How will you ensure that you won't segregate men but instead motivate and empower them for leadership and service churchwide?

- Count the cost—How many staff hours, volunteer hours, and dollars will it take to start this ministry?

- Promise not to overburden the staff—How will you be self-reliant (as a team)?

- Clarify responsibilities and authority—Who can leaders come to if they have a problem or concern about the men's ministry?

- Express benefits—How can you demonstrate that a healthy men's ministry will strengthen the whole church?

- Commit to forming alliances—How can you work with other ministries and departments?

You may want to organize your information in the following format. Be sure to leave a written copy with each leader you meet with.

Purpose: Develop a team to equip lay leaders who will implement innovative and relevant initiatives that minister to men of all ages.

Approach: Use a core team to lead and direct a process that will define and implement a new ministry strategy to serve men through discipling, mentoring, and coaching at all life stages.

Time frame: Allow yourself three to five years.

Initial tasks: Have weekly meetings with core team, monthly meetings with church leaders, develop program and activity ideas, and identify leaders and participants.

Request: List any necessary church office work space, access to conference rooms, administrative support, and other resources you might require.

5. Formulate a Battle Plan

George Washington, Norman Schwarzkopf, Tommy Franks. These great generals were known for what they accomplished— designing and implementing creative battle plans to win wars. Now that you've received your church leadership's blessings, it's time to call your command unit together and devise your ministry battle plan. But just what does a men's ministry battle plan look like?

Start with your objectives. Pull out your notes, and review and refine what you want to accomplish. Keep in mind the directives given to all Christians:

- "Go and make disciples of all nations."

- "Be filled with the Spirit."

- "Love your neighbor as yourself."

While these will likely be part of what you're all about, make sure that your ministry's objectives are unique and appropriate to your church. And be specific. General McArthur had a wonderful battle plan for the Philippines, but it wasn't transferable to taking Baghdad in 1991! And the 2003 charge on Baghdad was unique to those troops and that time! What does God want to do where you are right now?

Refine your vision statement. Revisit your objectives and flesh out how you'll accomplish the objectives with realistic goals. Some specific goals might include:

- publishing a men's monthly e-mail newsletter.

- establishing a network of small Bible study groups.

- hosting quarterly large group events.

Now that you've established clear goals, you can put together the task force you need to accomplish your mission. With your core command unit, define the ministry areas and types of task force members you'll need. Consider the following areas:

- marketing/publicity
- outreach
- event planning
- logistics

Before you start inviting men to lead in these or others areas, do you know what you want them to do? Define the roles and responsibilities for each area. State your leadership team's hopes and expectations.

Now you can invite other men to join your team—creating another level of leadership. As you broaden your base, don't overlook the qualities of teams. Great teams are

- *relational.* Do everything together, never alone. This is tough for many men. Establish a unit mentality rather than that of an army of one.

- *authentic.* Keep things real and practical. Be real with each other. This will happen only if it starts at the top.

- *intentional.* Always act with purpose.

- *united.* Be as one. This should be easy for Christians who are following Jesus, but don't be surprised if it takes a lot of work!

- *focused* on the long-term. Orient yourselves to the joy of the journey, keeping your thoughts on the process of *becoming* rather than simply *doing*.

6. Set Up Base of Operations

Now it's time to get organized! As you expand your team of leaders and workers, remember that organizational structure is just a tool that needs to be in sync with your vision so you can accomplish your ministry objectives. It helps you do what you do—it's not who you are. Before you start drawing boxes on a chart, review who you are as a men's ministry and make sure your organizational structure reflects that. Check your thoughts with these questions:

- Are you and your leaders in sync with the key values of the ministry?
- Do you have consistent prayer cover?
- Does each task and proposed activity or program relate to your mission?
- Does your structure encourage teamwork?

- Is what you're about personal?

- Do you provide levels for growth?

Note: If you're starting a men's ministry in a smaller church, you might be frustrated by now. You're picturing a men's ministry in some mega-church with dozens of jobs all mapped out on an organizational chart. Here's a thought that might help: Boxes on charts don't have to represent people. Instead, think of the different boxes as assignments or multiple hats that your key leaders wear. You don't need to assemble a team of fifty men to start an effective ministry.

You'll probably determine that you need to cover most of the following areas, depending on the manpower and resources you have available.

Oversight. As the name states, the oversight leader is responsible for overall ministry direction, supervision, and ultimate decision making. This is the person we've been calling the commander. With a servant's heart, he oversees the ministry to men, ensuring proper leadership development and team building.

Strategy. This person or team is responsible for focusing on strategic (overall, long-term) issues of the ministry. He helps define branding, themes, and priorities at the ministry level.

Coordination. This team of men offers advice about the overall direction of the ministry. They help define ministry objectives and priorities. This team would include the command unit—the initial core leadership team. They help establish what each of these organizational units will accomplish and provide direction to team leaders.

Prayer. This team intercedes for people, plans, and activities for men. They provide prayer cover and are available to pray with other teams.

Connecting. Members of this team actively welcome and greet individuals at men's functions. They also provide follow-up and coordination for people interested in getting involved in other areas of ministry.

Communication. This team puts together and distributes information for men. This includes creating promotional material for ministry events, newsletters, e-mail messages, Web site postings, database maintenance, events scheduling, and coordinating communication for men's meetings, projects, and teams.

Relationship. This team helps men deepen their spiritual maturity and build genuine friendships. They coordinate community groups, put together mentoring relationships, and explore approaches for discipleship and spiritual formation.

Resources. This group maintains lists of speakers, books, and other resources for men. They coordinate training and workshops.

Events. This team plans and organizes functions, gatherings, retreats and events.

Support. Members of this team take charge of general maintenance-facility setup and teardown; coordinating rooms, delivering equipment, and providing technical/media support.

Outreach/service projects. This team plans and coordinates community outreach and other short-term service-oriented projects.

R & D. This group researches and develops new ideas for ministry to men.

Adventure. This team takes charge of outdoor experiences, such as hiking, hunting, and sports.

Team leaders. Finally, these guys are the backbone of the ministry, the in-the-trenches leaders who make ministry happen. If you create a team of people for each of these organizational areas, you'll appoint team leaders to direct the teams' activities. The team leader's responsibilities include:

- serving as primary point of contact for the team.

- recruiting and connecting team members.

- organizing team meetings.

- communicating team status to the oversight leader.

- coordinating with other teams.

- setting objectives based on the battle plan.

- providing guidance to team activities and delegating tasks as appropriate.

- recruiting an assistant leader and developing new leaders over time.

- walking with God and caring for his team.

Present team leaders and members with a job description listing responsibilities for that area. Be specific! You'll find sample job descriptions for some of these positions on Toolbox pages 52-56.

Before you move on from your organizational structure, give some thought to how all of the men in these areas will communicate with each other. You need to be clear about the flow of communication—or it won't. Think through these important channels of communication:

- to your church leadership

- to the senior pastor and pastoral/ministry staff

- to the core leadership team/command unit

- among coordinators or team leaders of men's ministry areas
- prayer needs to anyone willing to pray for men's ministry
- to the men of the congregation

7. Recruit

You're finally ready to ask more men to join you on the mission! It's time to recruit your coordinators or team leaders for the organizational areas you just created in the previous step. Consider the following qualities before you start recruiting:

Passion. Look for men who believe in the importance of men's ministry and who have a passion for a particular area of ministry.

Gifting. If a man's heart is that of an evangelist, be sure to plug him into your outreach area. Beware of trying to recruit men by their current careers, where they've volunteered in the past, or by "seniority." You might want to use a spiritual gift inventory. See Toolbox page 57 for a list of online spiritual gift assessments.

Once a potential leader completes a spiritual gift inventory, he should ask three people who know him well and who've seen him serve in a ministry setting to answer the following two questions as a way to confirm the results.

- As you've observed me serve in ministry roles, what three gifts have you seen evident in me?
- What areas of service do you think I should stay away from?

Integrity. Just as the biblical standards for elders in 1 Timothy are high, the standards you set for leaders in men's ministry also need to be high. From ethical business practices to moral purity, you want the men in your church to respect the leaders of the ministry. This probably doesn't require a perfect past, but deal with any hint of a current lack of integrity.

Humility. This characteristic is embodied in a servant-leader. He understands that meekness is strength and serving others is leadership. Look for the man who will wash another man's feet. In the twenty-first century, this might be the man who is just as comfortable cleaning toilets as he is leading a large group.

Maturity. Look for a teachable spirit, a willingness to serve others, and a desire to grow personally and in relationship with others. How long someone has been at the church doesn't always equal maturity— some new Christians mature quickly and some longtime Christians are still spiritual babes. Physical age doesn't always determine maturity either—don't overlook young men who might need just a little nurturing and training in leadership. At the same time, don't neglect older and wiser guys who have experience and vision.

Personal style. Someone's personal style isn't necessarily a qualification for leadership, but understanding that style will enhance your ability to work together as a team. Check out Toolbox page 58 for several online personal style assessments potential leaders can complete.

Time commitment. Be careful to search out men who have time to lead. While there's some truth to the statement that busy people can get more done, it's also true that busy people can easily be overcommitted. Your team may be better off with an available leader than a famous name or a flashy character.

Expectations. When you approach potential ministry leaders, it's important that you can clearly state your expectations. That should be fairly easy to communicate using your base of operations—the organizational structure and job descriptions you worked on with your leadership team. But you should also be able to express what these platoon leaders can expect from you. Consider the following:

- Prayer support. Provide real intercession not before the meal "quickies."

- Vision. Give them a target to hit. "Where there is no vision, the people perish"—and your leaders are set up to fail.

- Availability. Be available and approachable.

- Training. Think creatively about ways you can grow the leaders on your team.

- Support with difficult situations. Stay in touch so you know when these are occurring.

- Logistical support. Grown men have "gone missing" for several weeks just trying to navigate the minefields of the church office. Help them out!

Remember that you're modeling leadership. Whatever your platoon leaders can expect from you, they'll offer to the guys they're leading. If your desire for your ministry leaders is to be praying, caring, people-oriented leaders, be sure you demonstrate that in your relationships with them.

Commitment. The final recruiting step is agreeing to work together. This means working through tough times together, laboring side by side with integrity and passion and caring. It means fully supporting each other and staying faithful to God and the mission he's called you to.

How do you find the right guys to recruit as leaders? Ask God who he is raising up to be part of the team. God will stir the hearts of different men. Some may be the pastors or staff of the church. Most will probably be laymen. Sure Passage recently conducted a survey of ninety-five churches that have growing men's ministries. More than 75 percent of these churches reported that their men's ministry was led by a volunteer rather than a paid pastor or staff member. That's exciting! You're involved in a grassroots movement—a movement of God.

8. Train

Training is like placing the proper tool into your leader's hands. Your leaders will want to be released to accomplish their ministries, but no one wants to be released unprepared! Think outside the church box. Be creative! Look for ways to equip and train your leaders. Look for seminars in practical areas. Investigate speakers who can sharpen the skills and motivation of your leaders. Network with other churches that are farther along in men's ministry. How can their leaders mentor your leaders?

Stretch the vision of your ministry leaders! Dream big! Look for ways to share with other churches the things you're learning. Work to develop training that provides hands-on content and at the following levels.

Individual level improvement and enrichment. Start by developing an orientation system to educate your leaders on the basic components of your men's ministry that you defined in the preparation phase. Encourage current leaders to work with an apprentice leader for a period of time. The apprentice shadows the current leader as he carries out his role within your ministry.

Group level interaction. Again, use group training times to introduce potential leaders to the ministry by communicating the basic components of the men's ministry you defined in the preparation phase. You can also bring in trainers who can teach basic leadership techniques such as meeting facilitation, activity/event planning, and coordinating follow-up. You can also provide training within specific areas of the men's ministry, such as current types of ministry outreach or how to schedule church facilities.

Organizational level. To aid with ministry-wide coordination and cooperation, provide initial and ongoing training that draws your entire team together. Here are a few suggestions:

- team kickoff meetings
- annual leader retreats

- quarterly training sessions on major themes
- monthly fellowship gatherings

Spending time together as a team will help you get to know each other. But have you ever noticed that a bunch of guys watching the same football game don't know each other any better by the end of the game? As you intentionally build authentic relationships in your team, you'll find some of these activities helpful.

- Share stories about an earliest memory, first leadership experience, first date, first car, or favorite meal.

- Pray for one another.

- Brainstorm ideas for activities that will deepen existing relationships or that have an outreach focus.

- Get away and be intentional about how you spend your time together as a group.

9. Deploy

Now that you've got leaders in place and have provided some basic training, it's time to release them to lead. Again, keep in mind that the ways you release and empower your leaders will be the model for the way they release their own.

Set up a leader kickoff meeting. Casting the vision—and making sure you're all on the same page regarding the vision—is the primary goal of this meeting. As the commander, you'll be responsible for setting the tone. Be positive. Encourage your men. Welcome each one. Demonstrate grace if things go wrong.

The great thing about releasing your teams is that they can put together pilot projects to actually carry out their area of ministry to and with men. Some of these projects will fail. Some will be wildly successful. And others will lead to a better idea. Coach your teams through these projects with the following ideas in mind.

- Dream—Think outside the box.

- Implement—Define the details, and make them happen. Keep in mind the purpose statement for the men's ministry and for your specific team.

- Refine and adjust—Honestly assess the outcome in light of your goal. Note ways you can improve or adapt in the future.

- Celebrate—Remember this is about the journey. So if you work together and try something new, and no one else shows up—is that a loss? No way! You dreamed, you tried, and you've strengthened relationships with your time as you shared the journey. There's no such thing as waste in God's economy.

Adapt on the battlefield. Any good commander understands the importance of making adjustments in the midst of battle. You've created a vision statement, organizational charts, job descriptions, and more. But they're just tools to accomplish the purpose. Don't focus on the tools so much that you lose sight of the purpose! Be flexible and ready to move if an opportunity comes up to bless, confront, or reach out to someone in a unique situation.

10. Assess Progress

How will you know if you're hitting your mark? Since laser-guided smart bombs are probably overkill, let's try something less technical. Question your leaders, and have them talk to the men that their area of ministry touches. Here are some simple questions to ask any man in your church:

- Are you involved in men's ministry? How?

- If so, what benefits are you receiving?

- How would you improve our men's ministry?

- If you're not involved, what would it take for you to try us out—not because you feel obligated but because you get something out of it?

These simple questions not only help measure your progress and growth, they communicate to uninvolved guys that the church has a men's ministry and they might be missing out on something.

Beyond just asking, it would be great to conduct a congregation-wide survey after your men's ministry has been up and running for a year or two. See Toolbox page 58 for a men's ministry questionnaire you can copy or adapt for your men's ministry, as well as a follow-up script you can use to call guys for additional information.

You'll also want to do team-specific evaluations periodically. These should be informal and "shoulder to shoulder" rather than "face to face." No one has to perform to meet someone's leadership standard. You're a team working together. Your evaluation asks, How's the team doing?

Finally ask for input from your team on how you're doing in your leadership capacity. How can you serve them better? What are you doing well? What could you improve on? You'll be amazed at the great ideas others have. A secure leader adjusts on the field.

11. Enhance Tactics

Through God's guidance, your leadership team will implement many ministry activities. Just as soldiers mature and strengthen through battle, your team can enhance its approaches over time. You'll find new ways to join ranks, charge and take new ground, set up camp and hold ground, and regroup when needed.

Here are a few ideas that your team can tackle.

- Conduct a brainstorming session on the primary life issues that men face.

- Ask the women's ministry in your church to list what they'd like to see take place in the hearts and lives of men.

- Visit a men's prison to minister to inmates, and observe firsthand the destructive patterns of wrong behavior.

Use findings from these and other events in your community to deploy new initiatives within your men's ministry.

12. Hone Tools

It would be much easier if the process of developing leaders and a leadership team was a one-time process. While you might concentrate more time on some of the early steps when you first start your men's ministry, chances are that you'll take all of these steps a number of times during your time of command. That's expected, because the process of leadership development is a constantly turning cycle. While you'll naturally become adept at adjusting on the battlefield, you should also take some time to adapt and improve these tools so they're finely crafted and customized for your church. Much of this chapter has focused on how to do men's ministry, with a number of tools you can duplicate. You're equipped to do this!

You may want to develop other tools as well. Consider how your team can create the following tools on its own.

- Keep track of contact information by creating a men's database.

- Provide team notebooks or folders so that leaders can keep ministry info up to date and consistent among the command unit.

- Employ effective communication by using personal phone calls, printed invitations to events, e-mail reminders, printed newsletters, and e-mail newsletters.

- Hold productive meetings by following established rules of conduct to honor and value one another's time.

- Listen to feedback by taking appropriate actions, making necessary changes, and following up with those who gave the feedback.

- Set behavior standards by dealing with difficult personalities, grumbling, and sin.

In case you think you're finished, here are some additional areas you'll need to develop your own tools for.

- interpersonal skills
- conflict resolution
- planning
- time management
- change/transition management
- attrition and replacing leaders

It's clear that you have an enriching but challenging job ahead of you. May God bless you as you hear his divine call to arms and as you call the troops around you to accomplish the eternal work of the kingdom.

Gentry Gardner

Gentry Gardner is founder and president of Sure Passage in Colorado Springs, Colorado, a ministry serving churches through interactive workshops, adventure experiences, short-term missions, life coaching, and team building for men's ministry. He also leads the men's ministry at Woodmen Valley Chapel in Colorado Springs. Gentry enjoys the outdoors and is always ready to blaze a new trail. He's been married for twenty years and is the father of three sons.

Visit his Web site at: www.surepassage.org.

CHAPTER 2 TOOLBOX

Sample Job Descriptions

Position

Oversight Leader

Purpose

Serve as commander of the men's ministry leadership team, not in a dictatorial style but in a biblical servant-leader manner.

Primary Responsibilities

Provide overall vision for the church's men's ministry; recruit other men to join the men's ministry leadership team; give direction and guidance to other men's ministry leaders; schedule, plan, and lead meetings of leadership team; empower and unleash men's ministry leaders to creatively lead and minister in their areas of responsibility.

Reports to...

Senior Pastor or Adult Ministry Director

Time Required Each Month

Depends on the size of church and men's ministry, if the ministry is just beginning or if it's already established, and the number of events the ministry holds annually. The time required could range from one to more than ten hours per week.

Term

If the men's ministry is just starting, the oversight leader should commit to a term of two to three years and consider renewing that commitment for a year or two after the initial start-up period. If the ministry to men is already established, this can be a commitment of two years—one year as an apprentice to the preceding oversight leader and one year as the oversight leader.

Training

Work as an apprentice to the previous oversight leader; attend fellowship or denominational leadership conferences, as well as regional and national men's ministry conferences.

Qualifications, Skills, and Gifts

Commitment to allowing God to work in his life; desire to use qualities and gifts wherever God desires; senses a call to lead ministry to men; gets energized by leading others; possesses gifts of leadership, administration, and encouragement.

Benefits

Gain a better understanding of the issues men face and find personal satisfaction while serving in this leadership capacity; work and form deep relationships with other God-honoring and committed men in the church.

Position

Events Coordinator/Team Leader

Purpose

As men search for places to test the waters of men's ministry, this leader will provide various entry points where both newcomers and seasoned attendees feel comfortable, connected, inspired, and transformed.

Primary Responsibilities

Coordinate the planning and carrying out of programs, special events, projects, and other activities; integrate a variety of events (breakfast fellowships, small groups, retreats) into connected and meaningful programs; ensure that events line up with both men's ministry vision and overall church vision; create new events (outreach events, guest speakers, adventure activities, father-son/daughter events, sports outings); work with Communication Coordinator to publicize upcoming events of the men's ministry; plan, organize, lead, and evaluate each activity or delegate these tasks to a team of equipped leaders as the ministry grows.

Reports to...

Men's Ministry Oversight Leader

Time Required Each Month

Depends on size of church and men's ministry, if the ministry is just beginning or if it's already established, and the number of events the ministry holds annually. Could range from one to more than ten hours per week. As the ministry grows, the Events Coordinator position will become a Team Leader position, overseeing coordinators/leaders of different men's ministry events.

Term

If the men's ministry is just starting, Events Coordinator/Team Leader should commit to a term of two to three years. If the ministry to men is already established, this can be a commitment of two years—one year as an apprentice to the preceding Events Coordinator, and one year as the Events Coordinator.

Training

Work as an apprentice to the previous Events Coordinator; identify needed training and communicate to Men's Ministry Oversight Leader; attend appropriate fellowship or denominational leadership conferences, as well as regional and national men's ministry conferences.

Qualifications, Skills, and Gifts

Commitment to allowing God to work in his life; desire to use qualities and gifts wherever God desires; senses a call to plan events that will draw in men and minister effectively to them; possess gifts of administration, leadership, encouragement, humility, and evangelism.

Benefits

Gain a better understanding of the issues men face and find personal satisfaction while serving in this leadership capacity; work with and form deep relationships with the leadership team and with other God-honoring and committed men in the church.

Position

Communication Coordinator/Team Leader

Purpose

To promote the events and ministries of the men's ministry through personal contact, newsletters, e-mails, Web site, brochures, bulletin boards, signs, displays, artwork, and photos.

Primary Responsibilities

Advise and assist other men's ministry leaders with their communication and promotional needs within the congregation; coordinate the scheduling, writing, and creating of all forms of communication; distribute communication pieces; maintain ministry database; oversee ministry publicity tools.

Reports to...

Men's Ministry Oversight Leader

Time Required Each Month

Depends on size of church and men's ministry, if the ministry is just beginning or if it's already established, and the number of events the ministry holds annually. Could range from one to more than ten hours per week. As the ministry grows, the Communication Coordinator position will become a Team Leader position, overseeing coordinators/leaders responsible for communications and promotion of different events and activities.

Term

If the men's ministry is just starting, Communication Coordinator/Team Leader should commit to a term of two to three years. If the ministry to men is already established, this can be a commitment of two years—one year as an apprentice to the preceding Communication Coordinator and one year as the Communication Coordinator.

Training

Work as an apprentice to the previous Communication Coordinator; identify needed training and communicate to Men's Ministry Oversight Leader; attend appropriate fellowship or denominational leadership conferences, workshops, and seminars on publicity, marketing, promotions, and public relations; attend regional and national men's ministry conferences.

Qualifications, Skills, and Gifts

Ability to communicate and work well with others; a willingness to lead and assist in all areas of communication and promotion for men's ministry events and activities; ability to listen; experience with reporting; possess gifts of administration, encouragement, and helps.

Benefits

See results of service as increasing numbers of men get involved in men's ministry events and activities; find personal satisfaction while serving in this leadership capacity; work with and form deep relationships with the leadership team and with other God-honoring and committed men in the church.

Position

Connecting Coordinator/Team Leader

Purpose

As new men become active in men's ministry, it's important that they feel welcome and integrated into various activities and relationship building events. The Connecting Coordinator works to ensure that these needs of individual men are met.

Primary Responsibilities

Strengthen the bonds among men in the church by connecting them to appropriate spiritual and social groups within the men's ministry and in the overall ministry of the church; gather and maintain accurate information about group members; assess current spiritual, relational, and emotional needs of men.

Reports to...

Men's Ministry Oversight Leader

Time Required Each Month

Depends on size of church and men's ministry, if the ministry is just beginning or if it's already established, and the number of events the ministry holds annually. Could range from one to more than ten hours per week. As the ministry grows, the Connecting Coordinator position will become a Team Leader position, overseeing coordinators/leaders responsible for connecting manageable numbers of men into appropriate groups, ministries, and places of service.

Term

If the men's ministry is just starting, Connecting Coordinator/Team Leader should commit to a term of two to three years. If the ministry to men is already established, this can be a commitment of two years—one year as an apprentice to the preceding Connecting Coordinator and one year as the Connecting Coordinator.

Training

Work as an apprentice to the previous Connecting Coordinator; identify needed training and communicate to Men's Ministry Oversight Leader; attend appropriate fellowship or denominational leadership conferences, workshops and seminars on assimilation, as well as regional and national men's ministry conferences.

Qualifications, Skills, and Gifts

A people person with good organizational skills and the ability to work with others; well-developed interpersonal and social skills; management skills of planning, directing, and communication; willingness to develop relationships with other men beyond the surface level, yet work largely behind the scenes rather than up front; ability to delegate and enable others; possess the gifts of administration, helps/serving, wisdom/discernment, counseling.

Benefits

See results as increasing numbers of men find relevance in the church and in their own lives by plugging in to appropriate groups and places of service that meet their emotional, relational, and spiritual needs; find personal satisfaction while serving in this leadership capacity; work with the leadership team and with other God-honoring and committed men and form deep relationships with them.

Position

Outreach/Service Project Coordinator/Team Leader

Purpose

To help the men's ministry reach out and share God's love with others through outreach activities, service projects, and mission opportunities; to work toward the goal of seeing more people come to make a faith commitment to Christ as Savior.

Primary Responsibilities

Gather and maintain information on opportunities to serve others—within the men's ministry, within the church, in the local community, nationally, and globally; coordinate and connect men to help meet these various needs.

Reports to...

Men's Ministry Oversight Leader

Time Required Each Month

Depends on size of church and men's ministry, if the ministry is just beginning or if it's already established, and the number of outreach events and projects the ministry desires to hold annually. Could range from one to more than ten hours per week. As the ministry grows, the Outreach/Service Project Coordinator position will become a Team Leader position, overseeing coordinators/leaders responsible for various outreach events or activities and service projects.

Term

If the men's ministry is just starting, Outreach/Service Project Coordinator/Team Leader should commit to a term of two to three years. If the ministry to men is already established, this can be a commitment of two years—one year as an apprentice to the preceding Outreach/Service Project Coordinator and one year as the Outreach/Service Project Coordinator.

Training

Work as an apprentice to the previous Outreach/Service Project Coordinator; identify needed training and communicate to Men's Ministry Oversight Leader; attend appropriate fellowship or denominational leadership conferences, workshops, and seminars on local outreach and missions; attend regional and national men's ministry conferences.

Qualifications, Skills, and Gifts

Organized; good listening skills; ability to delegate, desire to see others make a faith commitment to Christ; possess gifts of service, helps, administration, and giving.

Benefits

See results as increasing numbers of men seek ways to be involved in outreach and service projects; work with and form deep relationships with the leadership team and with other God-honoring and committed men in the church; experience personal satisfaction and inspiration as men work to bring others to Christ and as others make personal commitments to Christ.

TOOLBOX
Assessments

Online Spiritual Gift Assessments

☐ Natural gift test at On Target Ministries (15 minutes):
   www.otm.org/ginteractive.asp
☐ Modified Houts spiritual gifts test (30 minutes):
   buildingchurch.net/g2s.htm
☐ One local church's spiritual gifts test that works well:
   www.calvarychurch.ca/neatstuff/spiritualGifts/

Online Personal Style Assessments

☐ DISC Profile:
   www.discprofile.com
☐ Personal Style Indicator:
   www.improvenow.com/Assessments/CRG/psi/index.cfm
☐ Learning Style Assessments:
   www.mapnp.org/library/prsn_dev/lrn_styl.htm

TOOLBOX
Questionnaire

Men's Ministry Questionnaire

Your individual responses and personal information will remain confidential. Please complete and return this questionnaire today.

1. Select the five most important issues you think we should address in the next year. (Please number from 1 to 5, with 1 being most important.)

___ Spiritual growth
___ Bible knowledge
___ Evangelism
___ Missions
___ Mentoring
___ Marriage
___ Fathering
___ Friendships
___ Sexuality
___ Physical fitness
___ Life purpose/calling
___ Job/career
___ Finances
___ Time/priorities
___ Male passivity
___ Emotional balance (anger, fear, hopelessness)
___ Domestic violence
___ Pornography
___ Substance abuse
___ Other: _____

2. Check *one* primary area of ministry you'd be willing to serve in:

☐ Prayer (interceding for activities and people)
☐ Communication (newsletter, database, e-mail)
☐ Welcome (greeters, telephone follow-up)
☐ Planning (programs, events, administrative support)
☐ Facilities (setup, cleanup, technical support)
☐ Relationships (connecting, groups)
☐ Personal growth (one-to-one discipleship, mentoring, coaching)
☐ Training (teaching, equipping, modeling)
☐ Mobilize (coordinate involvement in each area)
☐ Other: _____

I'm willing to be the point man (primary coordinator/team leader) for this area:

☐ Yes ☐ No

TOOLBOX
Questionnaire

3. Your name: _____

4. How should we contact you? (Complete and check all that apply.)
Mailing address:

_____
_____

Would you like to receive periodic updates on ministry to men?
☐ Yes
☐ No

E-mail address: _____

Would you like to receive our men's ministry e-newsletter?
☐ Yes
☐ No
☐ Already receive it

Home phone: _____
Work phone: _____
Cell: _____

Please check the best way to reach you:
☐ Home
☐ Work
☐ Cell

Please check the best time to call:
☐ Morning
☐ Evening
☐ Anytime

5. Your birth date _____

6. Are you married?
☐ Yes
☐ No

7. Total number of children _____
Number of children living at home _____

Permission to photocopy this page from Men's Ministry in the 21st Century granted for local church use. Copyright © Group Publishing, Inc., P.O. Box 481, Loveland, CO 80539. www.grouppublishing.com

TOOLBOX
Follow-Up

Men's Ministry Questionnaire—Follow-Up Script

Important: Please call each guy on your list within the next week.
(This is just a guide to get you started and to have some consistency in the questions we ask.)

"Hello, this is _____ calling from _____ Church to follow-up on the questionnaire you filled out last weekend. Am I catching you at a good time?

First, I'd like to make sure that we have accurate contact information from you. [*Note: Based on how readable the form may be, check the following: name, address, e-mail, phone numbers, birth date, marital status, and number of children.*]

I see that you checked your primary area of ministry service as _____ [*Note: Areas of ministry include prayer, communication, welcome, planning, facilities, relationships, personal growth, training, and mobilization.*] Would you tell me a little bit about your interest in this area?

[*Note: Try to determine how long the man has been a Christian, the number of years at church, and any specialized areas of training.*]

Are you currently involved in other ministries at church?

Approximately how much time (during an average week) do you have available to work with us in ministry to men?

If we provided you with guidance and training, would you be willing to be the point man or assistant point man for the ministry area?

Do you have any suggestions on how we can be more effective in our ministry to and through men?

[*Note: If you have time, ask the following.*] I noticed the top two men's issues (out of five) that you ranked as most important were _____. Can you tell me why those stood out to you and if you have any ideas about how we should address them?

Is there anything that the men's ministry leadership team can be praying with you about? [*Note: Take time to pray if appropriate.*]

The last thing I'd like to tell you is that we're planning to schedule an information and planning session for all men's ministry volunteers within the next couple of months. Please keep an eye on the bulletin, and we'll also try to contact you directly.

Thank you so much for taking the time to talk with me today. Let me give you my name and phone number in case you think of any additional questions or comments you may have. [*Note: Give name and phone number.*]

Goodbye.

ENTRY POINTS: MORE THAN A PANCAKE BREAKFAST

When the pastor of a nearby church was called away on a family emergency one weekend, his church board called to see if I could preach at the Sunday services. I found the street and the church and then noticed a large sign out front: "All Welcome: Sunday Services—10 a.m."

Glad that I'd made it on time, I went inside to meet the deacon who had called me. While the sign in front read that all were welcome, a quick scan of the congregation revealed that about three-fourths of those who accepted the invitation were women. The prayers, readings, offering, and music—all confirmed that the sign should have read: "Women Welcome, Men Beware."

While the congregation was singing, "Jesus, oh Jesus, Come and fill your lambs," I decided to change my message. This church needed to hear that the gospel has a masculine side to it.

The Sunday morning service is the primary entry point for nearly every local church. But is the Sunday service a true entry point for men? Is it a safe place for men to be introduced to the gospel? Is it a relevant place for men to see that God has a plan for their lives? Is it a place where they can come as they are and experience a masculine Christianity? Is it a place where they can enter into safe and significant relationships with other men? The answers to these questions at most churches are no, no, no, and no.

While the typical (or even unusual) Sunday morning service isn't a great entry point for men, it doesn't mean your church can't provide positive entry-level events for men. Let's look at how you can accomplish that.

Goals of Entry-Level Events

Before you start putting together a whole calendar of events in the hope that you'll draw in men from your church who are currently uninvolved in your men's ministry, let's look at three goals any entry-point event or activity should accomplish.

■ Goal 1: Relationships

Several years ago, our church took ninety men to a Promise Keepers conference in New York. This was during one of the peak years for PK. While getting men to go was still a bit of a challenge, it seemed like a pretty easy invitation. Tens of thousands of men from the Northeast attended the conference, and it really inspired the men of our church. We felt like we were part of something. The question was, What were we part of?

That summer more than half of our men accepted an invitation to be part of a small group of men. It was great! Our men's ministry leadership understood that small groups would be the ideal place for men to grow and change. People—including men, of course—change in the context of relationships, and nearly all of the men in our church said that they didn't have a significant relationship with any other guy.

We also learned that this is pretty normal for men. That year a national men's ministry that I worked with had conducted a large-scale survey, and the results I saw reflected that only a small percent of men had what they would describe as "a best friend." Often, a man knows what a best friend looks like because he's had a friend like this in college or in the military, on a sports team, or during his high school days. But he no longer has a trusted friend like that in his life.

When the summer ended and our fall church season kicked in, many of the men who'd said they wanted to be in a small group were now backing out from that commitment. By the time we headed into the new year, only a minority of men who had attended the PK conference were still in men's small groups. What happened?

We made some mistakes. One very clear mistake was how we put our small groups together. We'd recruited leaders and then put together the groups on the basis of "convenience." We wanted to make it easy for our guys to say yes to a small group, so we gathered men by

- day of the week;

- time of day;

- geographic location; and

- book, topic, or Bible study.

This didn't work. There were some exceptions, but we'd made the mistake of assuming that men would make a relational commitment to guys who they really didn't know. The PK conference helped us identify the men in our church who wanted to be in deeper relationships. But we should have created a whole variety of safe entry points for men where they could get to know each other. Then as the men got acquainted with one another and our leaders at entry-point events, they'd receive a personal invitation from an emerging friend who'd invite them to join a small group—on the basis of relationship rather than convenience.

We've learned our lesson. Now when we invite men to be part of a small group, we do six things:

1. We invite them to be part of a new small group from the very beginning.

2. We let them know that no day of the week or time of day has been decided.

3. We let them know that no location for the group meeting has been decided.

4. We let them know that no book or topic has been decided on.

5. We affirm each of them as a friend.

6. We let them know when the small group will end (a clear exit point).

When we do an entry point for men, we now run the event through a grid of questions that includes: Will this event help me get to know someone else so that he might accept an invitation to be part of a small group?

■ Goal 2: Relevance

That same year another survey result I saw produced yet another interesting response. The men surveyed were asked to describe their local church experience. Two words came up more than any others. Two words from men who not only attend church but also accept the invitation to attend a national men's conference! Before you read what these men said, think about what word or phrase you'd use to describe your experience in your local church.

The two words from the men who were surveyed that came up most often were *boring* and *irrelevant*. Can you say, "Ouch"? How did this happen? How did the typical local church—which is largely pastored *by* men and has leadership primarily *of* men—end up becoming boring and irrelevant *to* men? What do men mean when they say the local church is boring and irrelevant? Let's start by looking at the definitions of those two words:

- *boring:* tiresome, tedious, dull

- *irrelevant:* having no bearing on the matter at hand

Could it be that when these men, who'd attended a huge conference in a massive stadium with fifty thousand other men, were asked this question, they didn't think of the overall ministry of the church but only of the Sunday morning worship service? A caring Christlike community that is mission minded and serves as God's representative on this earth is neither boring nor irrelevant. But the weekly service at the building where the typical church meets might be described with those words.

We've already stated that Sunday morning probably isn't an effective entry point for men. So in our churches, we need to intentionally develop entry points for men outside of the Sunday worship service that are interesting and relevant to men.

What would be interesting and relevant to adult men? Let's start by defining the terms:

- *interesting:* exciting the curiosity and holding the attention
- *relevant:* bearing to the matter at hand, pertinent, timely

The last few years I've had the opportunity to serve as a presenter for Great Dads fathering seminars. These four-hour seminars in local churches equip men to be great fathers and grandfathers. Why are the seminars successful? I believe it's because they're interesting and relevant—men want to be great dads! These seminars address the matters at hand in a man's life. They hold a man's attention because they engage him in an area of life that's extremely important to him.

When you plan an event that you hope will draw new guys into your men's ministry, you need to think about what will intrigue a man's sense of curiosity and be timely and pertinent for a man in your church. If the event is content driven, will the content address an area relevant to the life of an adult man?

■ Goal 3: Return

How do you overcome the inertia in men? That's the question Man in the Mirror ministries asks when addressing how to create momentum in your men's ministry. Many men aren't moving forward in their spiritual lives. As you lead and develop your ministry to men, your challenge is to help guys move from their prolonged state of rest to ongoing growth and change. Not an easy task!

As pastors and other leaders have worked hard at providing ministry to men over the last decade, what's resulted? While there are exceptions, the results are usually a series of starts and stops. Churches experience a short season of success followed by a longer season of failure. They see men come to an event, a conference, or a series of seminars, but they're not able to keep the interest of men.

The starts and stops in ministry to men may be due to disconnected entry points, bad timing, poor quality, and poor leadership. One common reason: not paying attention to the return that an event could bring to the ministry. What does that mean? It means that if you and your team work hard to put on a first-class entry-level event for men, you want to make sure there's a tangible return for your work. This is just good stewardship!

This return can and should look different for different events. Some examples might include:

EVENT	RETURN
Baseball game	50 percent of men succeed in bringing a guest.
Fathering seminar	Dads begin to read the Bible to their children.
Regional men's conference	Every man makes a real connection to another man.
Men's breakfast	Men who attend will come to the next breakfast.
Service projects	Men serving together.
Sunday school class	Men commit to pray once a week for other men.
Men's retreat	A four-week follow-up group offered for the men who attend.
Four-week follow-up	Two out of three men accept an invitation to a small group.

Ministry to men is too difficult not to give focused attention to a planned and prayerful return. Whether the events you design as entry points for men are providing a return, think through these questions:

- How does the event fit into your men's ministry calendar?
- Will the event launch what you're planning next in your ministry to men?
- Is there a specific result that can come out of the event?
- Will the visibility and reputation of the men's ministry be enhanced because of this event?
- Will new men come to know the Lord or the church or one another because they attended this event?

Don't be afraid of thinking about getting a return for your investment simply because you don't normally use those terms in a church setting. You're not looking for a financial profit; you desire to reap a spiritual profit as you help more guys be brave enough to enter into relationship with one another.

Six Issues When Planning Men's Events

What's different about planning events for men than for other affinity groups in your church? One thing that's different is that men are starting in different places than other people in the church. Let's look at some of the unique circumstances twenty-first century men are in, why these cause them to stay away from your ministry events, and what your men's ministry can do to overcome these situations.

1. Men Aren't in Relational Networks

My wife, Barb, was helping host a women's tea at the church. We arrived at church early on Sunday morning so she could post some details of the upcoming event on a white board in the church lobby. She wrote that it was a women's tea, the date of the event, when it started, what women could bring, and to please bring a friend.

I love my wife and want her to succeed in her ministry endeavors. I reviewed what she wrote and offered what I thought were some helpful insights. I asked her, "When does the event end?" "Is there a theme for the tea?" "Will you have a guest speaker?" "What else will there be to eat?" Before I could ask another question, Barb stopped me short and graciously shared with me, "This isn't a men's ministry meeting. We like to get together!"

She hit the nail on the head! I was running the promotion of her women's event through my men's ministry grid. While many women have a propensity to gather and just need to know the time and a place, men need all the facts of an event and numerous reasons to attend.

Most men operate in isolation and don't network easily, especially just to build relationships. Few men will pick up the phone and call a buddy just to see how he's doing. I'm still waiting for that type of call.

Men need multiple reasons to commit to a men's event. Most men don't easily invite friends to join them at an event. We "keep our options open" and wait until the last moment to commit to an event. Our felt need to gather with other men is low, and we usually need a compelling reason to leave our families or work or hobbies to join other men at a men's event.

If you think men will come to an event primarily to experience the joys of Christian brotherhood, you may end up with time alone with God.

2. A Chasm Exists Between Church and the Rest of a Man's Life

Most men invest at least ten hours away from home five days a week at their work. This constitutes half of their waking hours and nearly all of their emotional, physical, and mental energy. As companies downsize, men (and women, for that matter) are working to survive; they're willing to make greater sacrifices than ever just to keep their jobs. Issues of business ethics and integrity, time demands, and dealing with the authorities in their lives consume them, and they don't know where to go for answers. The typical Sunday church service seems so far away for overworked and overstressed men, and they may never hear a message that relates to their life at work.

What a great opportunity this chasm presents for your men's ministry. Perhaps you could hold a weekday business lunch at your church or another place and encourage men from the marketplace to get together. Invite a guest speaker who is presently in the workplace and who can make connections between faith and real life. Men want to hear from other men who have tackled and succeeded in the arenas that they're battling in.

3. Reach Men's Hearts, Not Just Their Heads

It seems that we've succeeded in stimulating the minds of men who attend our churches, but we've failed to reach their hearts. Many men find it easy to keep God at a distance because only their minds are engaged. Their hearts just remain in "park" or "neutral," and it becomes more and more difficult to get them back in gear. In *Wild at Heart,* author John Eldredge says that the great call by our society to men today is to "be nice." But this challenge isn't nearly enough to capture and fan a man's passion.

What arouses passion in men? Discover this and you'll see a significant measure of success in your ministry to men. Maybe the passion is fathering or grandfathering. Maybe it's exploring the second half of life. Maybe it's personal and spiritual renewal.

One of the great challenges in ministry to men is navigating the eighteen inches between a man's head and a man's heart. Most men are cautious about opening up, yet being vulnerable is the only way their hearts will ever be engaged. The men on the edges of your church need to see the male leaders of your men's ministry and leaders of the church set the pace in becoming vulnerable. When a well-respected man in a leadership position goes first in sharing his heart issues, he opens the door for other men to follow. This is true in every setting, from small groups to large events. Men need models; they need to see that a man can openly share his heart and still be strong.

4. Most Men Have No Margin in Life

Men are busy, or at least they feel very busy—it's really the same thing. You can try to prove to someone that he really does have a fair amount of discretionary time, but you'll just be wasting your efforts. The only thing that counts is how men feel, and no matter what stage of life they're in, men feel busy.

Because most men see that they have so little free time, men's events must be worth their precious time. That's one of the reasons many guys will delay their decision about attending an event—they have to weigh whether it's the best use of their limited time. Something better or more important might come up, so they struggle with committing to anything early on. This isn't necessarily an issue of procrastination; it can be a genuine desire to use time wisely.

Men will almost always internally ask this question about a men's event, Is it worth my time? They're making their mental list, comparing the invitation to a men's event against the need to date their wife, spend quality time with their kids, tackle the chores at home, catch their favorite team on television, log in a few extra hours at work, or address an assortment of other pressing demands.

This lack of margin in the lives of most men probably means that we should consider doing less events for men and doing the remaining ones we tackle better. More on that thought in a bit.

5. We Allow Men to Be Spectators

The church hasn't given up on men. But you've got to question whether men are truly a part of the church's "target audience." Most churches focus on meeting the needs of those who participate and those who serve. I remember hearing that in most churches during the 1990s, 80 percent of the volunteers were women. No wonder one pastor shared with me, "We're going with the 'goers.' The women's ministry in this church is going somewhere."

God bless women in every church who serve sacrificially and who labor tirelessly for Jesus Christ. We'd certainly be in trouble without them. However, simply because women are available and willing doesn't mean we should release men to live as spectators. Perhaps we need to set aside some service opportunities specifically for men. Men need to be challenged with fulfilling their roles as the spiritual leaders in their homes, churches, and communities. It's a given that they'll feel inadequate, too busy, and not as qualified as many of the women in the church. But our challenge is to equip them for acts of service.

Some of your most effective men's events will grow out of the need to specifically equip men in their God-given roles. Our church recently encouraged men to attend a six-week series for husbands titled "Leading and Loving." The format was simple: three weeks on leading and three weeks on loving. Yet most of the sixty-five men who attended these early morning gatherings had never been exposed to the scriptural principles presented. Or if they had, it certainly wasn't with a critical mass of other men who were all struggling to be God-honoring husbands.

The professionalism of church ministries may also contribute to men becoming spectators. It's easy to see this in youth and children's ministry. The church trains, hires, supports, equips, and resources gifted people who teach the young people of the church. This is a good thing. But it can become so good that men no longer feel any "righteous pressure" to team with their wives in the spiritual development of their own children. Instead, they place the spiritual formation of their children in the hands of the gifted and trained people in the church. Your men's ministry can offer events that challenge this kind of thinking, and that will put some of the righteous pressure back on men to be active in the spiritual development of their families.

God has specific designs for men in their homes, churches, and communities. Many of these designs require the church to equip men in order for them to succeed. As a leader of men's ministry, make sure that some of your men's events challenge men to rediscover the role that God has called them to. Create a bit of discomfort so men will quit watching from the sidelines and get into the game God has for them.

6. It Takes a Team to Plan an Event

"Two are better than one, because they have a good return for their work: If one falls down, his friend can help him up. Though one may be overpowered, two can defend themselves. A cord of three strands is not quickly broken" (Ecclesiastes 4:9-10, 12).

This point is more about men's ministry leaders than it is about the men you minister to in your church. It's hard to fault a leader who loves God, whose heart and passion are in the right place, and who will take a great idea for a men's event and start planning and preparing it all by himself. But this is a huge mistake! God promises a good return for our work when we serve together. We share the load. We use our unique mix of gifts to complement one another. We protect each other from our weaknesses. We encourage one another. We pray together. And we believe in and worship God together.

Rarely is a men's event a flop when a team of men undertake the planning and preparation. Even if only a few men show up, those who work together will always have deeper and more rewarding relationships develop in the process.

Far too many times, a man with a good heart, great vision, and significant energy has walked away from a men's event discouraged and exhausted. He tried to pull off the event by himself, and although the logistics fell into place, no one came. Because he was alone in owning the event, he's now alone in feeling the failure.

Men have a natural tendency to "do things themselves," but don't let any leaders in your men's ministry labor alone. Rescue the individual by coming together as a team around him.

Here's what a men's event team might look like:

- The team leader is the visionary and champion of the event.

- The logistics planner handles major items like the budget, setup, and food.

- The program coordinator manages the content flow and event specifics.

- The promotion coordinator organizes the marketing of the event.

- The promotion assistant helps the coordinator promote the event (you can never have enough help here).

If you're the leader who desperately wants to pull off a certain event—even if you have to do it alone—make sure you pause and think through what you're doing. If God doesn't raise up at least a couple of other guys to help you, perhaps it's not the right time or maybe something else will better serve the guys in your church. Make it a point to believe that God can give a diverse team of men the same passion before you tackle the planning and preparation of a men's event.

Five Lessons to Live By

We've covered a lot of ground here. We've looked at how your ministry can offer entry points for men that the typical Sunday morning church service can't. We've explored three goals your ministry should adopt when it draws in men through entry-level events. And we've investigated six unique issues that men face today, issues that make them pause about committing to participating in your ministry's events for men.

At each stage, we've offered some practical suggestions for overcoming the reluctance some men demonstrate for getting involved. But let's explore some more solutions, even some "against the grain" thinking that can help you draw more men into the starting points of discovering deeper relationships with other guys and with God.

1. Do Fewer Events and Do Them Better

Sometimes success can lead to excess. Picture this: A team of men puts on a great event to draw in the men of their church, and the guys actually show up! The organizers are surprised at the turnout and the buzz about how great the event was. "This must be it! This is what works in our church!" So immediately they begin to organize several similar events.

Problem is, it's too much and too much of the same for the guys in the church to support. Eventually the men stop coming and what was once a true entry-level event for men has turned into a small group of the same men.

The most common example of this is the Saturday breakfast for men. Several years ago, I called 110 churches in the New England region and asked them two questions.

Question 1: "Do you have a men's ministry?" Of the 110 churches I called, 102 said yes.

Question 2: "What does your men's ministry look like?" Of the 102, 78 said "men's breakfast." Most of those were held one Saturday per month.

When I had the opportunity to dig a little deeper, I learned that in most churches, fewer than 20 percent of the men at church Sunday morning would ever come to a Saturday men's breakfast. And because most of these churches are relatively small, it meant that many of these monthly breakfasts probably had an attendance of ten or less guys. Here are few observations on the typical church Saturday morning breakfast for men.

1. Ten men or less is a large small group and not an entry-level event for men.

2. For an event in which you're just trying to get guys to taste men's ministry (and some soggy pancakes), once a month happens pretty quickly in most guys' schedules.

3. Thanks to the good guys from church who get up a little early one

Saturday a month to cook these breakfasts (maybe eggs of some sort, white toast, and coffee). But what about that menu is going to attract someone new?

4. What's the purpose? How does the monthly breakfast connect to other events and activities of the men's ministry? How does this month's breakfast get-together connect to last month's breakfast get-together? Speaking of connection, why should a brave visitor return next month?

5. It's not easy to plan and prepare something *good* every month.

So let's look at some ways to improve the typical Saturday breakfast for men.

1. Encourage the monthly group of men to continue meeting monthly as a small group, but don't promote it as a place for newcomers to discover what men's ministry is about.

2. Start a new quarterly breakfast that you promote to every man in your church. Follow the rules for promoting an entry-level event: Overkill men with facts about the event so they hear many reasons to attend. Give the starting time, the ending time, details on who's speaking, the menu, the theme, and how the breakfast fits with other events in the men's ministry.

3. Make the meal worth the drive. You can still offer great guy food, but find a gifted cook—male or female—or go hire a caterer!

4. Develop an annual theme, and bring in speakers. Don't forget to explain how these events will deal with the major heart issues men are facing, and offer hope for winning the battles!

5. Find a different champion for each quarterly breakfast. Just four guys with passion who will each lead the team once a year.

These adjustments bring the following big changes:

- You do fewer breakfasts.

- The breakfasts you do are better.

- There's less ongoing labor involved.

- The men who had met monthly can continue to meet.

- A true entry point is born.

2. Offer a Variety of Events for a Variety of Men

The old monthly men's breakfast can never touch the majority of men in your church. More and more guys work on Saturdays. Dads are active with their kids on Saturdays—soccer, baseball, hockey, music lessons, and a dozen other commitments. Vacations, family events, and other church activities compete for weekend time as well.

The purpose of an entry-level event isn't to get a guy to come to an event; the goal is to get the man connected to the men of the church. The event is a means to that end. This means that you need to develop a variety of different events that are of different spiritual intensities that meet at different times that will attract men with different interests who are all in different places in their spiritual growth.

While this may sound like it has the potential of becoming an overly busy ministry, keep in mind: Do less and do it better! Instead of a rapid-fire machine-gun approach, lay out a three- to five-year plan that provides a variety of entry points to reach a variety of men. It's OK if you don't reach everyone right away. Not everything needs to happen between September and June!

Low spiritual intensity. If you were to think of options for entry-level events for men based on spiritual intensity, what events do you think would work best at providing a nonthreatening spiritual environment? Consider the following events:

- golf tournament
- Valentine's Day banquet
- service projects to help out widows and single moms
- workday at church
- traditional summer cookout
- father-son campout
- father-daughter banquet
- movie night
- sportsmen's banquet
- wild-game cookout
- Super Bowl party
- Mother's Day brunch
- fishing trip
- softball game

Moderate spiritual intensity. Now let's turn up the heat a little. What about events that might be a bit more spiritually challenging to those who attend? Consider the following events:

- weekend retreat
- fathering seminar

- marriage seminar
- sexual-purity seminar
- Promise Keepers or another men's conference
- breakfast with guest speaker
- Sunday school class
- book discussion group
- Bible study

3. Make Entry-Level Events Safe

The low intensity entry-level events should be safe for most men—meaning that most guys with some church experience will feel comfortable attending. You'll have to work a little harder to make the other events truly safe. Here are a few hints to help make any event safe.

Have food. Men can sit together and talk as long as they have a purpose like devouring a roasted pig! They aren't at the event to deepen relationships. Instead, they show up for the fun or challenge of the event itself. However, some entry-level relationships (meaning conversation on the surface and just below the surface) will be a natural byproduct of eating and talking together.

Laugh together. Find something to laugh about. Find several things to laugh about. Most of us have lives that are already way too serious. Build positive memories, and give guys something to talk about later by providing opportunities to laugh together now.

Name tags. Unless your church is small, chances are most men can't remember the names of the guys around them. Help them out by providing name tags.

Quiet is OK. Quiet is even good. There can be opportunities at your event for men to talk. But outside of giving his name, occupation, and where he lives, no one should be forced to share his latest struggle or recite his favorite Bible verse.

Praying out loud. Prayer is great, but don't put any man in a situation where he must pray out loud. Don't force anyone to do something he doesn't want to—even pray out loud. Instead, designate one of your regular attendees to pray.

Ending time. This is something you can use to help promote your event. Make sure that everyone is aware of it. Communicate it again at the beginning of your event. Stick with it. Don't ask permission to extend the event.

Delay the follow up. You may want to use an entry-point event to build relational bridges so that you can invite a man to be part of a small group or to attend your men's retreat. But don't bombard the poor guy with too much at once. Instead, extend your invitation a few days later. This creates another mini-entry point!

4. Make Entry-Level Events Masculine

A men's event isn't just a church-sponsored event that only men attend. Instead, your planning and preparation should make sure that the event is distinctively masculine. Here are a few ideas to help that happen.

Men only. It's tough to pull off an event that's distinctively masculine if both men and women attend. I was asked to speak at a regional men's event a number of years ago in Connecticut. I arrived early and connected with a couple of friends who were hosting the event at their church. It looked very organized, and they were expecting a good crowd. I realized that there were quite a few women around the church, and I made the comment that it was nice of the women to volunteer and support the men's event. He shared that some of the women had asked if they could attend the event, and the men's ministry leadership said it would be all right. I pointed out that the program for the day specified "men's summit." While we had a good half day together, very little was masculine about our time together. The worship was sweet, the hall was pretty, and I had to change my message.

Most women understand that men need a time and a place for just men to come together. They know the special dynamic that exists when women gather, and they presume a similar dynamic occurs when men gather. There's no secret agenda; men aren't conspiring to take over anything.

Content. I had to change my message that day because it can be inappropriate to teach on some topics in a mixed setting. A couple of years ago, Vision New England Men's Ministries surveyed men across the Northeast and found that 63 percent claimed that sexual temptation was their number one temptation. This is an example of a topic that is distinctively masculine. Would it be proper to have any kind of significant men's gathering but not talk about what men call their number one temptation? I've seen God move in men's hearts to confess their sin and ask for God's forgiveness when they felt safe in a masculine environment. While this topic doesn't feel all that safe, the church must provide entry-level events for men that deal with real-life issues.

Setting. Promise Keepers conferences showed us that men worship differently, connect to other men differently, and respond to God differently when an event takes place outside the church. A man shows up at a basketball arena wearing a polo shirt and ball cap. He picks up a pretzel and a soda and finds a seat in section 221. He knows this place as he comes here to watch the local team a couple of times a year. He stretches out and waits for things to get started. He lets his guard down, and he brings all of his masculinity with him into this place.

However, you don't have to move every men's event outside the church to make them distinctively masculine. But if you do use your church's facilities, it might be helpful to move the event out of the sanctuary and into a fellowship hall or gym. The very simple goal is that a man will bring all of his masculinity with him when he attends the event.

Work to Get Critical Mass—Numbers Count!

One other dynamic that makes Promise Keepers conferences masculine is the number of men who attend. I attended my first PK conference in the summer of 1994 in Boulder, Colorado. I went reluctantly and had low expectations. I didn't value big events because I was more interested in using my time to disciple men. The conference was held in an outdoor stadium on a beautiful summer evening. It began with fifty-two thousand men singing "Holy, Holy, Holy"—and I knew that something special was happening! It was critical mass. I'd never worshipped God with thousands of men. I sang loud and with a full heart. The stadium was packed. The singing was loud. This was masculine worship. I wanted to duplicate that feeling back home. Here are a few ideas for accomplishing that.

Participate in your denominational or fellowship's men's retreats. Many churches hold their own retreats, renting space at a conference center and bringing twenty-five or thirty guys there for a night or two. This has good qualities but so does the idea of "bigger." Most denominations and associations have a regional retreat for men. It will gather several hundred men together once a year at a retreat center and bring in a first-class speaker—and the number of guys attending means you can sing loud and free during worship times!

Host or help plan and organize citywide or regional conferences. If your church isn't part of a denomination or association and you can't get to a national conference, work together with several churches in your area to host an annual men's conference. It might take a little more time and a higher level of cooperation and trust to develop these conferences. But once you get them started, these entry-level events can be a dynamic part of a church's ministry to men.

Recruit national presenters. Find future seminar presenters for your group by scouting out (via Web sites, tapes, newsletters, and conferences) dynamic regional and national men's ministries across the country. You can find contact information for many of these ministries at the National Coalition of Men's Ministries' Web site at www.ncmm.org.

Visible Ministry Leads to Invisible Ministry

Remember, the purpose of an entry-level event isn't to get men to come to an event but instead to get men connected to other men of the church. These events are the visible part of your ministry to men. They make the church bulletin and the Sunday announcements. These events show up on the radar.

But below the radar are a variety of ministry opportunities that are invisible to most people in your church. Small groups of men, Bible studies, mentoring, counseling, leadership training, and other nearly invisible forms of ministry are the real places where guys build deeper relationships, where leaders train and equip emerging leaders, and where men change the direction of their lives in newfound or renewed relationships with God.

Your men's ministry needs to plan for how the visible ministries will lead men into invisible ministries. If you don't take this step, your ministry to men will stagnate. Your entry-level events will lose momentum because it seems there's nowhere else to go once a guy is beyond "entry level."

Communicate "Facts" Guys Need to Make a Decision

Keep in mind that most men don't have a natural tendency to gather. You can't simply announce that the men of the church are getting together and then expect guys to join you. They want a number of questions answered before they'll even consider your invitation:

1. Why are you having the event? What's the purpose?

2. When is it?

3. When will it end?

4. Where will it be held?

5. How do you get there, and how long will it take?

6. How much does it cost? Is there a price break?

7. Is there a speaker—and who is he?

8. What do I need to bring?

9. Will there be food and beverage served?

10. Will I be asked to do something or join something?

Our church took a good number of our men to a regional men's conference in Syracuse one year. I asked two of the men from the church who didn't attend why they stayed home. I expected to hear that they had a scheduling conflict or something. Instead, they each had rather simple questions about the logistics of the weekend, but they never got around to asking about them. Our marketing was incomplete and didn't communicate all the facts these men needed to make a decision that was comfortable for them.

Give Every Man Five to Seven Touches

Men need the facts, and they need to hear them many times in many ways. Many women will hear about an event and check their calendars to see if they can go. Most men don't function this way. The average guy might not even check if he has something else going on until he becomes convinced that he'd like to attend the event. Men are different and you reach them in different ways. Be sure you develop a comprehensive plan to promote your event. Here are a few ideas.

1. Pray, and ask God to move men to the event.

2. Provide a brochure, and make sure the quality of the brochure represents the quality of the event.

3. Put up a poster—a man may not read a brochure, but he'll see the poster.

4. Design a bulletin insert—if his mind wanders during church, he may give it a look.

5. Send him a postcard in the mail to arrive at his home midweek.

6. E-mail him. Take the extra time to copy and paste and send him a "personal" e-mail.

7. Make use of your church's Web site. Provide every detail a man could ever need.

8. Clue in the women's ministry. Wives can give guys a *gentle* nudge as well as their blessings to attend your men's event.

9. Make use of a platform announcement. It will work best if the senior pastor says, "Please join me..."

10. Make phone calls. Organize a team of guys to call all the men in your church—don't overlook anyone.

Nothing Beats a Personal Invitation

A slick brochure marketing a superb event won't come close to the power of a personal invitation from a friend. This isn't just a phone call reminder from a man on the men's ministry team; this is one man asking another guy to go to the event with him.

It's important for men who serve as leaders in a church to understand this. With the other areas they're responsible for, church leaders can sometimes see an entry-level event for men as a low priority. It's critical that leaders understand their role in inviting other men to join them at entry-point events. When church leaders embrace a men's event and extend personal invitations to other men, the event takes on a life of its own. The reverse is also true. When the leadership of the church doesn't embrace a men's event, the promotional efforts will be a challenge.

Develop First-Class Printed Materials

Remember your audience! Many men in your church work with quality printed material and receive four-color promotional mailings and ads at home, yet printed material for church events gets duplicated on an out-of-date copier in a church closet. Right or wrong, this sends men a signal about the quality of an event.

Send the men of your church a different signal by budgeting funds for the design and creation of excellent brochures and posters. Find people in your church or hire outside professionals who have expertise, such as a graphic artist to create well-designed materials. You're competing for men's time against other church events; send every man a compelling message that the event will be worthy of his time.

Create Discounts for Early Registration

A men's event doesn't need to be free. In fact, most men believe you get what you pay for. If your event is free, how good can it be? Men pay to attend sporting events, movies, plays, seminars for work, and to go out to eat.

You can also help secure a man's attendance at an event by getting his registration fee up front. Most men are reluctant to throw money away. Men also like to get a deal. If you offer a good discount to register early for an event, you may find that guys will be quicker to sign up.

Create Continuity

Put together a whole calendar of events for men rather than a series of isolated events.

One men's ministry team had a good leadership team and a fair amount of momentum in their ministry. One year they developed a series of dinners designed to address the dangers that men face. Each month they highlighted an area: power, greed, anger, lust, competition, and isolation. The dinners began in January with more than a hundred men attending; by May, less than twenty men were coming. What happened?

While January is a good time to begin something, September is better. Use the summer to plant seeds, then begin the church year with your best efforts.

They promoted each month individually. This men's group didn't have speakers lined up for all the dinners, so the men decided not to create a brochure showing the entire schedule from January to June. They missed the opportunity to communicate continuity; instead, the dinners were communicated as a series of isolated events.

If men can see the prayer, planning, and preparation your leadership team has put into the events they're being asked to attend, they'll be more likely to participate. You communicate quality when your nine-month calendar for men's ministry is ready and distributed by Labor Day.

Develop a Tradition

An entry-level event could become a tradition. When people think of the men's ministry of your church, what comes to their mind? The answer to this question will help you understand if any event is becoming a tradition. When an event develops into a tradition, men and their families will put it on their calendars before the marketing even begins. Here are some examples of traditional events.

Annual men's retreat. One church has a winter ski retreat for men from Sunday to Wednesday. They rent a beautiful chalet, hire a top-notch chef, bring in a quality speaker—and go skiing every day!

Sportsmen's dinner. This kind of event will often draw men from both inside and outside your church. Men bring wild game to grill, and hear from a celebrity sportsman.

Guys Night Out. "First Monday" began at Grace Chapel in Lexington, Massachusetts a number of years ago. Men come for dinner and a speaker who addresses the annual theme. "First Monday" makes it easy to remember the date.

Service ministry. How about a team-based service ministry, maybe to help out single moms and widows? Men serve people with special needs and also develop meaningful relationships with a team of like-minded guys.

Learn From Every Event

What went right? What can we do better?

Men's ministry isn't an exact science. It's important for your leadership team to take time to highlight what went right at each event, as well as evaluating what you can do better next time. Be sure you establish clear goals for what an event is intended to accomplish to help you evaluate the effectiveness of your event when it's over. Ask God what he wants to do through your team and each event. Put your goals on paper and develop plans to accomplish them.

In fact, that's probably the best thing you can do for every aspect of your ministry to men. As you make sure that you're doing the ministry that God wants you to, your team will enjoy the process of serving and the privilege of co-laboring with one another.

Brian Doyle

Brian Doyle serves as director of men's ministries for Vision New England. He has a daily radio ministry for men called "Man 2 Man Express" that can be heard nationwide. Brian and his wife, Barb, and their five children live in West Hartford, Connecticut.

Visit his Web site at: www.man2manexpress.com.

CHAPTER 3 TOOLBOX

The Process of Building Ministry to Men

1. Start with the few.
- develop a leadership team

2. Develop a variety of relevant entry points.
- breakfasts, barbecues, sporting events, service days
- equipping seminars that specifically develop men
- Bible studies, adult Bible classes for men
- annual retreats, conferences

3. Develop small groups for men.
- closed
- open
- relational
- one-on-one

4. Develop men to follow Jesus.
- become men of prayer
- study and apply the Word
- deal with personal sin
- operate under the Lordship of Christ

5. Develop men who lead in the home.
- date, relate, communicate, and pray with their wives
- family nights, family devotions
- disciple their kids
- guard the gates of their homes

6. Develop men for service in the church.
- gift assessment and understanding
- actively engaged in a servant role
- supports the pastoral staff
- stewardship of time, talent, and treasures

7. Develop men for personal ministry.
- build friendships, find common ground
- identify with Christ, share their faith
- mentor another man
- facilitate a small group

8. Develop leadership in the local church.
- spiritual disciplines
- ministry skill set
- doctrine and theology
- character development
- personal maturity

TOOLBOX
Entry Points

Providing a Variety of Entry Points

When your men's ministry provides a variety of entry points, you make it easier for men to get involved. The men in your church are in different seasons of life and have different interests. How much they get involved will depend on their interest in spiritual things, their readiness, and the time that they have available.

Large Scale Events

Principle: These events act as a catalyst to motivate men and ignite local men's ministry.

Implications: Men make life-changing decisions at these events, and they come home ready for the next step.

Men's Special Events

Principle: These are the nonthreatening activities that allow men to become acquainted with each other. Special events can include barbecues, softball games, and fishing trips.

Implications: Special events are a great place for men to bring unchurched friends, new men in the church, or those not yet involved.

Men's Equipping Seminars

Principle: Seminars and training sessions offer men the opportunities to develop in areas that are specific to being a Christian man. Seminars on fathering, finances, sexual purity, being a God-honoring husband, career and time management, and anger are all good examples of equipping seminars.

Implications: In addition to serving as a good entry point, a seminar provides encouragement, practical tools, and training not found on Sunday morning.

Men's Congregational Gatherings

Principle: These are the events in the life of the church that give the men's ministry a rhythm. They are the weekly Bible studies, monthly breakfasts, and annual retreats that develop a loyal following.

Implications: Regular gatherings at your church or at a retreat site give men a taste of what can happen in a men's small group.

Men's Small Groups

Principle: Small groups offer a man the greatest potential for spiritual growth. He chooses to become a member of a team committed to mutual support. These groups thrive when they start with personal invitations, little details, and clear "exit" points.

Implications: Small groups help men overcome the isolation in their lives. They provide an environment where men can grow in Christ and where men can share how to minister to their families, friends, church, and communities.

Men's Ministry Evaluation

Check the statements below that best describe your men's ministry.

Purpose Statement

☐ We don't have a purpose statement for men's ministry.

☐ We have a stated but unwritten purpose statement.

☐ We have activities but not a ministry focus.

☐ We have a developed purpose statement with ministry-focused activities.

Leadership

☐ We don't have an identified men's ministry team leadership.

☐ We have one or two men who provide leadership to our men's ministry.

☐ We have developed a broad-based leadership team.

Small Groups

☐ We currently don't have men meeting in small groups.

☐ We have several small groups that are meeting regularly.

☐ We have many small groups that are meeting regularly.

Relationships

☐ We don't have accountability relationships developed among the men in our church.

☐ We have sporadic development of relationships among men; there is little accountability.

☐ We have seen strong, vital relationships develop among men in the church; there is high accountability.

Scheduled Activities

☐ We have one or two men's ministry activities a year.

☐ We have some regularly scheduled men's ministry activities each year.

☐ We have planned men's ministry activities to encourage men to participate at various levels of interest.

Outreach

☐ We are seeing little or no participation in our men's ministry.

☐ We are seeing some involvement in our men's ministry.

☐ We have a large number of men who are involved in our men's ministry and they're actively inviting others.

Impact on the Family

☐ We have a few men leading some form of regular family devotions in their home.

☐ We have many men who lead some form of regular family devotions in their home.

☐ We have men helping other men lead some form of regular family devotions in their home.

Impact on the Church

☐ We have a few men who are active and who are having an impact in the church.

☐ We have a core group of men who are committed to the pastor and the ministry of the church.

☐ We have a significant number of men actively supporting the pastor and involved in church ministry.

Chapter 4

GUYS MOVIE NIGHTS: NO GIRLS ALLOWED

For the past three years, a bunch of Christian guys in a little Colorado town have gotten together every few months to watch a movie, eat guy food, and talk.

Just don't tell them that it's fellowship.

That might ruin it.

"Guys Movie Night" started when Jack invited some guys over to his house on a Friday night. He told everyone to show up with a snack to pass around (classic guy food only—no vegetable trays allowed). It was low-key; they'd eat, watch a movie he'd rented, and then talk about what they'd seen.

What movie was Jack showing? He wouldn't say.

The movie was *Kramer vs. Kramer*—an oldie but goodie. And guys who'd known each other on the surface discovered they had *way* more in common than they suspected. Each had been touched by divorce in some way, and the movie prompted a powerful discussion.

They decided to meet again in two months, at Dan's house this time, to watch a movie Dan selected.

Thus was born the guys movie night.

Does a "Guys Movie Night" Belong in Your Men's Ministry?

Guys getting together to watch movies is nothing complicated—but it is worth adding to your men's ministry as an entry point.

Here's why.

▪ You Draw Men Who'd Never Attend a "Men's Ministry Meeting"

A movie every two or three months is a totally low-commitment introduction to building relationships with other men. Those attending aren't required to talk unless they want to, although most guys are comfortable enough to enter into discussion.

Think of a guys movie night as a threshold experience for men: It's a place where they can form relationships and start to build trust. It may be a steppingstone for more significant involvement in your ministry down the road.

▪ You Can Gauge Their Spiritual Condition

Because discussions delve into significant topics, men reveal glimpses into what they think, feel, and value. Oddly, a group of guys talking about priorities after watching *City Slickers* will probably say more than if the same guys were sitting in a Sunday school class.

■ Guys Take Ownership

Men who never lead anything else at church are able and eager to host a Guys Movie Night. The job description is simple:

1. Pick a time and place.

2. Select a suitable movie (more on this later).

3. Make sure there's enough Cheez Whiz to go around.

It's not rocket science.

Launching a Guys Movie Night

The most important thing to remember is that the point *isn't* to watch movies. The point is to set up discussions and encourage fellowship. The movies are simply shared experiences and discussion prompts.

That doesn't mean the movies you choose are unimportant. Screen a lame show at a movie night, and you'll likely endure mocking for a long time.

Here are eleven principles for ensuring the movie selection is appropriate, as well as other things you should know as you launch your own simple movie nights for men.

1. Meet in Homes

This is smart for several reasons, but foremost among them is "marketing." It's one thing for a married guy to say, "Honey, I'd like to go to the theater with some friends to view a film and then stop for dessert and discussion afterward." It's another thing to say, "Honey, me and some other guys from church are watching a movie in Harold's basement while we guzzle root beer and choke down beef jerky."

The first option sounds like something a wife might actually want to do with her husband. Not being invited to go along feels like a slight. But you couldn't pay most wives enough to sit in a basement eating disgusting processed food while watching a movie selected by some guy named Harold. Once they're sure the event isn't a bachelor party, most wives will happily give their blessing for their husbands to go—alone.

One thought: Once every year or eighteen months, it's good to catch a first-run movie in the theaters, then grab banana splits or pie afterward. A change of pace keeps things fresh.

The second reason it's smart to meet in homes is that the cost is minimal. A movie rental, snacks, and steam cleaning the carpet after someone spills chili-cheese dip is peanuts.

Besides (and this is reason three), when men are invited into each other's homes a bond forms. You could call it the "Brotherhood of the Basement."

Rotate hosts and homes even if Stephen has a fully integrated surround-sound home theater system with plasma monitor and Ryan has a thirteen-inch TV with vertical hold troubles.

2. Don't Announce the Movie's Title

If you announce the movie that will be screened, guys might decide to attend based on whether they've already seen the film. But a movie that wasn't impressive in first run, might still make a great discussion starter.

Remember: The movie itself isn't the point. Discussion and fellowship matter more, so let the suspense build. Reveal the movie title when everyone's plates are full and all the men are already parked in front of the screen.

3. Stick With PG or PG-13

You might agree to allow an occasional R-rated movie, but not if the rating reflects sexual content. Causing brothers to stumble isn't part of fellowship. Look for suitable movies in the PG range—there are plenty. There's always something in movies that might offend one person in your group. But a PG rating ensures that the offence will probably be minor.

A word of advice: Don't try fast forwarding past "bad" scenes or muting the sound. You can't be that quick on the trigger, and your attempt at censorship will probably destroy the viewing experience. It's better to not screen a movie than to attempt to clean it up.

4. Eat Basic Guy Foods

Ask men to bring food from the four basic guy food groups: fat, caffeine, sugar, and barbecue sauce. Having each attendee bring something to pass around is more than a way to ensure the host doesn't go broke—it also builds ownership of the event.

At one guys movie night, our host served freshly grilled trout. But that set such an impossibly high food standard that the next host despaired and served trays of Twinkies.

Some hosts cook hamburgers. Some order a couple of pizzas. None of them worry much about a balanced diet or cutting calories.

5. Don't Meet Too Often

My group meets just quarterly, but some of us connect at church and work between times. If you don't see the other guys in your group except at movie nights, you could meet more often—say, every month or two. Meet more frequently and you'll eat into guys family lives. Meet less often and you'll lose the relationships you're trying to build.

After discussion, set the date for your next movie night and pick a host before you leave. (Remember: Don't announce the movie.) Friday or Saturday nights often work best. E-mail a reminder (asking for an RSVP) along with a map to the host's house about two weeks before the event, and follow up with a final announcement two or three days before the movie night. That way, nobody can say he wasn't reminded.

6. Leave Women and Kids at Home

This is an exclusive event—guys only.

Is this sexist? Probably.

Does having this policy allow for deeper discussions? Absolutely.

7. Choose Movies Wisely

Consider adopting this policy: While the host decides what movie to rent, members of your group agree that movies need to fit the following criteria:

- The movie is PG-13 or tamer—unless there's a very good reason.

- The movie has been prescreened and scrutinized by the host.

- The movie is less than 2½ hours long.

- The movie has a thought-provoking theme and substantial spiritual and/or emotional content.

- The movie is one most of you haven't seen, at least not *lately*.

These filters effectively weed out recent blockbusters that most of you have seen, as well as racier movies. This still leaves a lot of options. Check out the "little films" that never saw national distribution in major theaters. Sometimes films created for HBO and other cable channels are excellent, too; however, they often aren't rated, so be careful.

If you're really brave, explore "chick flicks." These movies tend to focus on relationships and provide a lot of material for discussion.

Just expect to hear things like, "That *You've Got Mail* movie would've been better if Tom Hanks had just blown up Meg Ryan's bookstore in the first place."

8. Don't Use the Pause Button

Once the movie starts, it keeps rolling, buddy. If you have to visit the Little Boys Room, either hold it and do your business later or step out and miss a few minutes of the film.

Be wise and plan ahead.

9. The Host Controls the Remote

This is a matter of respect. You don't go into a man's home and kick his dog, do you? Then why do think you can touch his remote?

10. The Host Starts the Discussion

After the movie ends, it's part of the host's job to get the conversation rolling. The discussion may suddenly take a dramatic left turn once it starts, but the first nudge is up to the host.

For instance, after *Apollo 13* ends, the host might say, "How calm do you think we'd be if we knew there was a good chance we were about to die? What does that say about what we believe happens after death?" The discussion may eventually center on the way people react when under pressure at work—but the host got things going.

Three suggestions about leading a movie night discussion:

1. Don't let anyone dominate the conversation. This can happen several ways, so look for these personality types as you talk about the movie:

- The *therapist* is very comfortable with opening up (or expecting others to do so) in a group setting. This person may confuse the movie night with group therapy. He'll want to explore deep, personal issues at length and share poignant stories that illustrate his inner conflict. Of course, this will absolutely freak out the other guys in the group and send them screaming for the door.

  Gently let therapists know that while conversation at a guys movie night can—and should—dip beneath the surface, few men show up expecting to scuba dive with emotional or spiritual topics.

- The *evangelist* is always looking for a way to bring the discussion back to the need for Christ. While this isn't a bad thing in itself, a faith decision isn't the point of *The Truman Show*.

Remind evangelists that movie nights are about forming relationships. It's these growing relationships that give men permission to speak truth into each other's lives.

- The *jokester* isn't comfortable with getting personal, so he turns every comment made into a punch line. Eventually, this will shut down conversation—who wants to share anything when there's a good likelihood you'll be harpooned with a joke or lampooned as the butt of one.

  Refuse to play the jokester's game. Gently challenge his behavior—even pulling him aside away from the movie night, if necessary. Don't be dissuaded by the distancing humor.

2. Ask follow-up and personal questions. If Jack says he thinks Mr. Holland (in *Mr. Holland's Opus*) sold out for a paycheck instead of starving until he became a famous composer, you might ask, "How important is it to do something significant?" If Jack says it's very important, gently probe further by personalizing the next question: "It sounds like several of us agree, but none of us have written a famous opera yet. How important is it to do something significant before we die? What might that be? What would it be for you?"

3. Set some ground rules. After a few movie nights, your group will develop a rhythm for discussions. But it never hurts to put a few ground rules in place and review them occasionally. Here are some you should consider:

- This is a group discussion. Let's leave room for everyone to comment.

- It's OK to disagree but not to be disagreeable. Every point of view will be respected.

- No double dipping in the salsa.

That pretty much covers it. After the ground rules have been set, your group will probably be pretty much self-governing during discussion times. Men will probably challenge each other's comments but not in a demeaning or critical way.

11. Keep This Bonus Insight to Yourself

This question *always* works when the discussion is floundering: "Which character in this movie do you most closely identify with—and why?" Tuck that question in your wallet next to your emergency twenty-dollar bill, and don't pull it out until you're truly desperate.

The Movies

On the following pages is a starter list of twenty-one films with accompanying discussion starters. In addition, check out Toolbox page 108 for another thirty movie quick picks; for these, you'll need to come up with your own discussion starters based on the suggestions above.

Mikal Keefer

Mikal Keefer is a husband and dad living in Colorado. He's a founding member of a guys movie night and has never forgotten the night he screened a chick flick. "I nearly had to go into hiding," he says. "It's a mistake I haven't made twice."

The Sixth Sense (1999)

Genre: Suspense/Drama
Length: 107 minutes
Rating: PG-13 for intense thematic material and violent images

Plot

Dr. Malcolm Crowe, child psychologist, attempts to help a boy who claims to communicate with dead people—who don't know they're dead! As the therapy continues, Dr. Crowe discovers that his own view of reality might be flawed.

Discussion Starter Questions

- Describe a time you discovered that you'd been wrong about someone or something, or a fresh insight appeared in a flash. What did you learn? What impact did that have on how you felt or behaved?

- Dr. Crowe couldn't see what was really happening to him. How is that like being a Christian living on earth?

- Would Dr. Crowe have been happier staying ignorant of his real situation? Is ignorance really bliss? Why or why not?

Galaxy Quest (1999)

Genre: Action/Adventure/Comedy
Length: 102 minutes
Rating: PG for action violence, mild language, and sensuality

Plot

When cast members of a long-cancelled television show discover they've been taken seriously by a race of aliens, they get the chance to play out their TV roles in real life—and the stakes are high.

Discussion Starter Questions

- Describe a time you felt like a fraud—when you felt less competent than people assumed you were. What happened? How did it turn out?

- How does it feel when people express confidence in you?

- How does it feel when people express confidence in you, when they clearly *don't* have confidence in you?

- When it comes to living out what we believe, is it a good thing to act confident about our religious beliefs even if we're feeling doubt inside? Why or why not?

Groundhog Day (1993)

Genre: Comedy/Fantasy/Romance
Length: 103 minutes
Rating: PG

Plot

An abrasive weatherman named Phil discovers he's repeating the same February 2 over...and over...and over. Unfortunately for Phil, he's the only one who knows what's happening. He decides to turn—mostly by trial and error—February 2 into a perfect day.

Discussion Starter Questions

- If you could build a perfect day for yourself, what would it be like? What and who would be in it?

- If you could relive any one day of your life and try to improve it, what day would you choose? What would you do differently?

- Phil was a jerk that few people liked. He learned to change his behavior—or at least enough of it—so that Rita changed her mind about him. Do you think people fundamentally change? Why or why not?

The Emperor's Club (2002)

Genre: Drama
Length: 109 minutes
Rating: PG-13 for some sexual content

Plot

William Hundert is both principled and passionate concerning how he runs his classroom and the Classics he teaches. Until Sedgewick Bell and institutional politics appear, his system works well. But times change. Will Hundert change with them? And when faced with a difficult ethical choice, how will Hundert respond?

Discussion Starter Questions

- Sedgewick was a cheater in prep school...and as an adult. Do you think people can fundamentally change? Why or why not?

- What prompts true and lasting change in people's character?

- Hundert compromised his integrity, but he didn't confess until twenty-five years later. Was the confession a good idea? Why or why not? What does that suggest we might do about old hurts we've inflicted on others?

Mr. Holland's Opus (1995)

Genre: Drama
Length: 143 minutes
Rating: PG for mild language

Plot

Glenn Holland, a musician whose career is going nowhere, temporarily takes a teaching job until he can get his career as a serious composer on track. Years later he's still in the school band room, having found fulfillment in mentoring young musicians.

Discussion Starter Questions

- When you were a child, what sort of job did you picture yourself doing at the age you are now? If money were no object, what sort of work would you do now?

- Describe a time you started a job or project that you thought wasn't all that important—but you found meaning in it.

- In what ways could the job you're doing now be used by God to touch lives? What would that require from you?

October Sky (1999)

Genre: Drama
Length: 108 minutes
Rating: PG for language, brief teen sensuality, alcohol use, and for some thematic elements

Plot

Nothing in the coal mining town where Homer Hickam was raised encouraged scientific experimentation. So Homer's desire to build and test rockets was met with...well...a distinct lack of enthusiasm. Homer and several friends are determined to build a viable rocket and win scholarships through a science fair.

Discussion Starter Questions

- What have you wanted to do that you were willing to risk ridicule—and failure?

- What's a dream you've had that you were willing to work at to make real?

- Describe a time you stuck with something that was difficult. What was it? What happened?

Life Is Beautiful (1998)

Genre: Drama/Comedy
Length: 118 minutes
Rating: PG-13 for Holocaust-related thematic elements

Plot

An Italian Jew uses his sense of humor to win the heart of the woman who will become his wife. Later, during World War II, his humor and ingenuity serve to save the life of his son in a Nazi death camp. *Note:* In Italian, with English subtitles.

Discussion Starter Questions

- Guido, the protagonist, found beauty in simple things. Rank yourself from one to ten: to what extent do you do that in daily life?

- Describe a challenging time in your life. How did living through that period affect your ability to feel joy and to enjoy life?

- Do you believe God works through difficult situations in our lives? Why or why not?

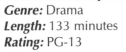

Quiz Show (1994)

Genre: Drama
Length: 133 minutes
Rating: PG-13

Plot

In the 1950s, a televised quiz show phenomenon turned the brightest contestants into instant—and wealthy—stars. It was a time of intellectual challenge, catapulting careers, and fraud. Based on a true story, this movie documents how the scam unraveled and how millions of viewers were duped.

Discussion Starter Questions

- It turned out that the quiz shows had no integrity. What institutions that impact your life do you view as having little or no integrity? Why?

- Suggest a definition for the word *integrity*. As a group, work to sharpen and combine your definitions. What's your collective definition?

- Why do you think God values integrity so highly?

Remember the Titans (2000)

Genre: Drama
Length: 113 minutes
Rating: PG for thematic elements and some language

Plot

A Virginia high school football team must integrate in 1971—and that includes the coaching staff. The transition isn't easy, but it does change lives—including the lives of the coaching staff, the team, and the town the school calls home.

Discussion Starter Questions

- Change—deep, heartfelt change—is often hard. What's an attitude or behavior you've changed? How did the process of changing feel?

- Racism is one theme of this movie. How has racism touched your life?

- Leadership matters on a football team just like it matters in life. How would you describe the leadership demonstrated in this movie? Why?

Kramer vs. Kramer (1979)

Genre: Drama
Length: 105 minutes
Rating: PG

Plot

Ted Kramer had no idea how to care for his young son—until Ted's wife, Joanna, walked out the door and didn't come back. Ted must discover how to care for his son and then, when Joanna reappears, how to fight for custody.

Discussion Starter Questions

- Divorce has touched most of us in some way. How has it impacted your life?

- As you watched Ted and his son, in what ways did it remind you of your own relationships with those to whom you're close?

- If you could snap your fingers and eliminate the possibility of couples getting divorced, would you do it? Why or why not?

The Apostle (1997)

Genre: Drama
Length: 134 minutes
Rating: PG-13 for thematic elements and a related scene of violence

Plot

"Sonny" Dewey is a Texas preacher who discovers his beautiful wife is having an affair with Horace, a younger minister. After assaulting Horace, Sonny disappears and starts over in Louisiana. He leaves his life behind but not his faith. This movie chronicles Sonny's path to redemption and his confrontation with his past.

Discussion Starter Questions

- Is the statement "Sonny was a faithful Christian" true or false? Why do you answer as you do?

- In what way does Sonny's faith journey remind you of your own?

- If you were able to pass sentence on Sonny when he's brought to trial back in Texas, what sentence would you give? Why?

The Truman Show (1998)

Genre: Comedy/Fantasy
Length: 103 minutes
Rating: PG for thematic elements and mild language

Plot

It's the ultimate reality show: on camera 24/7 for his entire life. That's what Truman Burbank experienced. But he never knew his town was a television set and everyone around him were actors. Then one day Truman gets suspicious...and the lie unravels.

Discussion Starter Questions

- Truman got quite a shock: He discovered his world was a lie. Describe a time you discovered that something you thought was true turned out to be untrue. What was it? How did you feel?

- Truman had to make a choice: Stay in the cocoon of his make-believe world or walk out into the unknown truth. What would you have done in his situation? Why?

- How is following God like the decision to leave the safety of a known world and move into an unknown one?

Chocolat (2000)

Genre: Drama/Romance
Length: 121 minutes
Rating: PG-13 for a scene of sensuality and some violence

Plot

This is widely considered a chick flick, but don't be fooled. When a single mother, Vianne, and her child move to a rural French village and open a chocolate shop, there are power struggles galore: between Vianne and the mayor, between the mayor and the new priest, and between a group of river-rafting free spirits and the local townspeople.

Discussion Starter Questions

- Which character in this movie evokes sympathy in you? Why?

- If you had to identify the most Christlike character in this movie, who would you pick? Why?

- Power and its use is a sub-theme running through this movie. Where did you see power being used well—and poorly?

Signs (2002)

Genre: Drama/Science Fiction
Length: 106 minutes
Rating: PG-13 for some frightening moments

Plot

When a five-hundred-foot crop circle appears outside his home, the Rev. Graham Hess finds his patience challenged. Why would someone be playing a joke on him? When the crop circles begin to show up all over the globe and alien spacecraft arrive, Rev. Hess' faith—already strained after his wife's tragic death—is further tested.

Discussion Starter Questions

- OK, 'fess up: Do you believe in extraterrestrial beings? Why or why not?

- If you knew for certain that other intelligent species existed on other planets, how would that make you feel?

- When Graham Hess lost his wife, his faith in a loving God was shaken. How has a loss affected the way you feel about God?

A Man for All Seasons (1966)

Genre: Drama
Length: 120 minutes
Rating: G

Plot

Sir Thomas More did the unthinkable: He stood up to a king. England's King Henry VIII wanted to divorce his wife and looked to the aristocracy for endorsement. Sir Thomas More found himself required to choose between standing for his principles—and facing dire consequences—or agreeing to the king's demands.

Discussion Starter Questions

- As a group, list eight to ten principles you think someone might be willing to die for.

- If you watched a man die for something he believed in, would that man strike you as a hero or a fool? Why?

- Describe a principle you hold that you believe you'd cling to—no matter what.

The Mosquito Coast (1986)

Genre: Adventure/Drama
Length: 117 minutes
Rating: PG

Plot

Allie Fox is a brilliant inventor, but stubbornly dogmatic in his beliefs about how to build a sustainable, better world. Allie suddenly takes his family to Central America, where his attempt to create a utopian paradise works well until he encounters obstacles in the form of a preacher...and armed thugs.

Discussion Starter Questions

- Allie is intellectually brilliant—no question about it. How might his life have been different had he been equally as gifted in relational skills?

- Allie was willing to give his all to fulfill his vision. What vision in your life would you be willing to give your all for?

- Allie and Rev. Spellgood quoted Scripture at each other but only to prove their points. How do you use Scripture in your life?

City Slickers (1991)

Genre: Adventure/Comedy
Length: 112 minutes
Rating: PG-13

Plot

Mitch, Phil, and Ed are middle-aged guys having midlife crises. Their solution: experience an action-packed, two-week cattle drive from New Mexico to Colorado. On the drive they meet Curly, a weather-worn trail boss who challenges Mitch to find the "one thing" in life.

Discussion Starter Questions

- As a general strategy for finding meaning in life, how does taking adventure vacations strike you? What else might you try?

- If you've reached or exceeded middle-age status, how are you handling the transition through those years? What do you suggest younger guys know or do to ease the transition?

- If Curly stuck his gnarled finger in your face and asked you to identify your "one thing," what would it be? Why?

Chariots of Fire (1981)

Genre: Drama
Length: 123 minutes
Rating: PG

Plot

British track athletes preparing for and competing in the 1924 Summer Olympics face obstacles of both a spiritual and physical nature. One of the runners is a devout Scottish missionary, and another is a Jewish Cambridge student. Both excel, but for very different motivations.

Discussion Starter Questions

- Running for God or running to make a point and for public applause—which strikes you as closest to why you dash through your day at work and home?

- Eric Liddell is held up as a role model in part because he's a famous runner. Do we do Christians who excel in public arenas any favors by making them role models? Why or why not?

- Eric Liddell stood firm on his principles, but at a cost. If you've done the same at some point in your life, share that story.

Hoosiers (1986)

Genre: Drama
Length: 115 minutes
Rating: PG

Plot

In Indiana, basketball is nearly a religion, and this tiny school never dreamed its team would be in the state finals. But it happened—and a legend was born. *Hoosiers* is based on a true story.

Discussion Starter Questions

- If you could be awarded the Grand Champion trophy for something in your life, what would it be? Why?

- The basketball players who won the state title were instant heroes. How well do you think you'd handle instant stardom?

- Describe a time you accomplished something that you or others thought next to impossible. What was your accomplishment? How did it feel?

The Family Man (2000)

Genre: Comedy/Fantasy
Length: 125 minutes
Rating: PG-13 for sensuality and some language

Plot

Jack Campbell is a fast-lane investment broker who hasn't a regret in the world. He's got it all: fast car, fast career track, and gorgeous girlfriend. Then one morning he wakes up to the life that would have been—that is, if he hadn't broken up with his college sweetheart. In this new life, he has kids, a van that won't start, and a decidedly less-than-spectacular career. For Jack, which life has the most satisfying rewards?

Discussion Starter Questions

- In many ways, this is a movie about values. How would you describe Jack's values? How do they compare with yours?

- If you had the opportunity to see how your life would have turned out had you made different choices, would you want to know? Why or why not?

- Coulda, woulda, shoulda...decisions we made long ago sometimes haunt us. If there's one of those in your past that you're comfortable sharing, what is it? How would you make that decision now?

Les Misérables (1998)

Genre: Drama/Crime
Length: 134 minutes
Rating: PG-13 for violence and for some sexual content

Plot

Jean Valjean was sentenced to nineteen years in prison for stealing bread. After being paroled, he stole silverware from a bishop who fed him a meal. Caught with the stolen goods, Jean is astounded when the bishop forgives him and gives him more silver to bankroll a new life. After becoming a successful businessman, Jean is identified as a parole-breaking ex-convict by a policeman who once served as a prison guard. Jean disappears but is hunted by the policeman.

Discussion Starter Questions

• How significant was the bishop's forgiveness in the life of Jean Valjean? What evidence do you see in Jean's life to support your answer?

• The policeman believed in rules and regulations; Jean seemed to value grace and forgiveness. Which character most resembles you?

• Who in your life has demonstrated acceptance and grace? How has that affected how you live your life?

CHAPTER 4 TOOLBOX

Movies to Never, Ever Show at a Guys Movie Night (And We Really Mean It)

The Straight Story (1999)

Great concept, interesting message, deep story, and rated "G." But slower than a lawn tractor oil leak.

Any Complete Trilogy

They take too long and usually only die-hard fans enjoy an overdose of anything—even Middle Earth.

Any *Portion* of a Trilogy

If there's back story that must be explained, it interferes with the viewing experience. Resist temptation.

Most Christian Films

If there's too obvious a message, the movie will be mocked. Remember: You're screening it in front of a group of critics who are just waiting for a chance to trash the movie you've so carefully selected.

Any Movie Featuring a Purple Dinosaur or a Talking Tomato

TOOLBOX

Thirty Quick Picks: Movies Worth a Look

Here are some additional movies you may want to consider for Guys Movie Night.

1. *Tender Mercies* (1983)
2. *The Ten Commandments* (1956)
3. *Ben-Hur* (1959)
4. *The Count of Monte Cristo* (2002)
5. *On the Waterfront* (1954)
6. *A River Runs Through It* (1992)
7. *Sergeant York* (1941)
8. *I Confess* (1953)
9. *The Hiding Place* (1975)
10. *The Mission* (1986)
11. *Luther* (2003)
12. *The Passion of the Christ* (2004)
13. *Saving Grace* (1986)
14. *The Fourth Wise Man* (1985)
15. *To Kill a Mockingbird* (1962)
16. *Brother Sun, Sister Moon (Fratello Sole, Sorella Luna)* (1973)
17. *Cape Fear* (1962)
18. *Apollo 13* (1995)
19. *Rudy* (1993)
20. *Lord of the Flies* (1963)
21. *Pay It Forward* (2000)
22. *Keeping the Faith* (2000)
23. *Unbreakable* (2000)
24. *Mr. Mom* (1983)
25. *O Brother, Where Art Thou?* (2000)
26. *A Beautiful Mind* (2001)
27. *Searching for Bobby Fischer* (1993)
28. *Finding Forrester* (2000)
29. *The Skulls* (2000)
30. *Dances With Wolves* (1990)

Section 3

GET MEN TO CARE ABOUT EACH OTHER

Chapter 5

Relationship Building: Beyond "I'm Fine, How Are You?"

by Tim Doyle

Chapter summary: How to make deep and intentional relationships a foundational part of your ministry to men.

Chapter 6

Bible Studies: Into the Word and Each Other's Lives

by Gary Wilde

Chapter summary: Ten ready-to-use Bible studies to help men deepen their relationships.

Chapter 7

Retreats: Boys Just Want to Have Fun

by Jim Neal

Chapter summary: Practical steps for planning men's retreats that will draw guys into meaningful and lasting relationships.

RELATIONSHIP BUILDING: BEYOND "I'M FINE, HOW ARE YOU?"

Late one Sunday afternoon a few years ago, I rushed into the house to answer the phone. On the other end of the line was a distraught Jesus. It wasn't really Jesus—it was the man playing Jesus in our church's annual Easter drama, which I was directing.

We'd had a rehearsal earlier that afternoon, and he'd expressed some strong disagreements with the way I was portraying the Last Supper scene. Now on the phone, he was still upset. When I asked him to explain his concerns, he danced around the issue for a few sentences. When I pressed further, he finally blurted out, "I don't want to play a *gay* Jesus!" Surprised, I inquired what direction I'd given that gave him that impression. "You want me to *hug* the disciples when we leave the table," he said in disgust. "Jesus would *never* have done that!" And with those words my "Jesus," who also happened to be an elder in our church, defiantly quit our Easter drama.

Besides creating last-minute chaos for me, this story illustrates how far we have strayed from biblical principles for appropriate man-to-man relationships.

Why would it be difficult to picture Jesus strongly embracing each of his disciples as they said their final goodbyes at the Last Supper? These were men he walked with, ate with, instructed, discipled, rebuked, and shared life. And this would be the last time he'd see his companions through human eyes before enduring the agony of the cross. I find it much harder to imagine their departure marked by stiff handshakes and an exchange of business cards! Just moments before, John the Beloved leaned against the chest of the Master at the dinner table—certainly that must have violated someone's personal space!

Up Close and Personal

Would you call Jesus weak or effeminate? That's not the image Scripture portrays of the man who tossed tables in the Temple, rebuked storms, and fought toe-to-toe with Satan himself. At the Last Supper, the same Jesus modeled a relationship so transparent as to strip down, strap on a towel, and proceed to wash the dusty feet of his friends. Why is this demonstration of affection between close male companions so foreign to us today? Answer that question and you'll understand why my reluctant actor was so outraged at the thought of the Master displaying tenderness toward those he loved. And I don't think this is an isolated case: I've seen men refuse to return to a couples' Bible study group after having to hold hands with another man in a mixed-gender prayer circle.

Something has gone seriously awry with our definition of what constitutes "normal" male contact and appropriate closeness among men friends today. It's also a sad commentary that the church offers little demonstration of the genuine article that God intended for men to experience through strong masculine friendships. We need a new standard of normalcy—or, more accurately, a return to a biblical standard—when defining how men relate to other men.

The Father Vacuum

To recover the kind of relationships God meant for us to enjoy with each other, let's begin by examining what prevents us from being able to pursue these connections. If we learn how men relate to other men primarily by watching our own fathers, then many of us didn't have the best of examples as we were growing up of what masculine friendships look like. Consider that nearly 24 million children (about 34 percent) in the United States live absent from their biological fathers. About 40 percent of children in father-absent homes haven't seen their fathers at all during the past year; 26 percent of absent fathers live in a different state than their children; and 50 percent of children living absent from their fathers have never set foot in their fathers' homes.[1] These numbers don't even take into account the millions more children whose fathers are emotionally absent—the father lives in the home but is emotionally disconnected from his children. In light of these statistics, it's no surprise that we're experiencing the devastating effects of what sociologists call the "father vacuum." Beyond these numbers, nearly all of us have been affected by this vacuum in one way or another—there are no perfect fathers.

Both the father vacuum and the household vacuum serve the same purpose—*they suck dirt.* In an effort to feel macho, in control, and good about ourselves as men, we allow anything and everything that crosses our paths to get sucked into our lives: power, money, abuse of others, alcohol, pornography. All of these problems, to one degree or another, grow from our feeble attempt to compensate for the genuine article. When the vacuum sucks garbage into our lives that doesn't belong there, we must turn to the only source able to legitimately fill the void in our lives—the *only* perfect Father who ever was or will be.

Jesus provides the model for what every man needs to walk in wholeness. At his baptism the Son of God comes up from the water, the heavens open, a dove descends, and a voice speaks—the Father's voice. What does the Father say to the Son at this significant moment? "You are my Son, chosen and marked by my love—*pride of my life*" (Luke 3:22, *The Message*, emphasis added). Wow! You can almost hear the buttons popping off the Father's shirt as his chest swells with pride. Talk about an affirmation! If such acknowledgement from the Father was important for the *Son of God* to hear, how much more vital must it be for us.

Observe the backdrop of God's statement: Had Jesus done any miracles yet? Had he healed any sick, raised any dead? No. His Father's affirmation was based solely on relationship, not performance! In the same way, we must also receive our identity from the Father—whether or not we ever get it from our earthly fathers—in order to escape the pull of the vacuum. Then, from that position of strength and confidence, we can pass his blessing on to those around us.

Why is this so important? Because this gaping tear in the fabric of society is the perfect opportunity for the church—perhaps through dynamic ministries to and among men—to take the lead in bringing healing to ourselves, the men around us, and their families.

Wading Into the Deep Waters of Relationship

With this basic understanding of the issue that keeps us from enjoying close male friendships, let's look at some steps we can take to experience, model, and lead others into the blessing of strong masculine friendships.

■ Filling the Vacuum

I am convinced that healing the father vacuum is the core issue facing men in the church today. (Women, too, for that matter.) I've watched seventy-year-old men, pillars in their church with grown children, grasp the reality of this issue and tell me, "I had a man in the home when I was growing up, but I never had a *father.*" Even after decades of living, these men still yearn for the approval and confidence they never received from earthly fathers. How can a man ever hope to operate in strength as an effective husband, father, and friend of other men from such a weakened position?

Before we can hope to have healthy and satisfying relationships with others—including our parents, wives, children, and our brothers in Christ, we must confirm our identity in relationship with God. We must first connect with *the* Father. Without that core identity issue settled, we'll run and hide from intimate relationships with other men, afraid of the rejection we might experience. Or we'll wrap our inadequacies and insecurities in false bravado, and seek to obtain power and superiority over others through domination and intimidation. Both pathways are unhealthy and counterproductive to experiencing healthy, intimate male friendships.

Even after experiencing healing in this area of my own life and ministering to men on this subject for years, I'm still tempted in times of insecurity to look to others around me for identity, approval, and affirmation. The truth is that we're only free to fully enjoy close male relationships when our own wounds have been exposed and healed. That process begins by asking Christ into your life, confessing your sin and weaknesses to him, and submitting to his Lordship over *all* things—including the wounds of your heart. Only then can you experience a true relationship with *the* Father, followed by deeper relationships with those around you.

■ Surrendering the Scars

Even after we give Christ control of life, a process remains that we need to walk through. Of course, God can choose to sweep away some of the difficulties in our lives in an instant, but many issues require a lengthier journey involving the people around us. For many of us, *forgiveness* is key to receiving God's fullest blessing in our lives. There comes a point when we need to decide if we'll forgive those around us for the hurts they've caused us. Whether this means forgiving our earthly fathers, our Christian brothers, or others who have caused us pain, we can either bleed to death through the wounds they've caused, or—like the wounds Jesus endured on our behalf—we can allow God to use our pain to bring life to others. God's plan is to set us free so that that we can become agents of healing to those around us. Rather than use our past as an excuse for poor choices in life, we can choose to allow God to heal our wounds and, in turn, be vessels of healing to others.

It all sounds so clear-cut, doesn't it? Just get healed, get over it, and get on with life. Of course, it's usually not that easy. I've often prayed, "Lord, why don't you just take this pain away from me?" The answer to that question is always the same—I can almost hear God reminding me, "If I took away the things you struggle with, you wouldn't need me anymore, would you?" God often leaves struggles and wounds in our lives so that daily we have to choose the narrow path that builds the resistance, patience, and stamina we need to make us stronger Christian men. This must be what Paul was referring to when he prayed three times for God to remove a struggle in his life. God's answer each time was, "My grace is sufficient for you."

One final thought concerning scars. Long after a wound heals, a scar remains. The physical scars on our bodies are visual reminders of painful episodes in our lives. Emotional scars carry the same kind of memories; even years later, the scars can be just as sensitive as the original wounds.

In the movie *Shadowlands*, Anthony Hopkins in the role of C.S. Lewis utters an amazing line. After the death of his wife following a bitter struggle with cancer, Lewis reflects on the pain by surmising, "As a boy I chose safety. As a man I choose the pain, knowing that the pain of today is part of the joy to come." Avoiding the pain of life is to avoid life itself! Through the process of surrendering your scars, you can learn how to walk free from one-dimensional "cardboard" living and embrace the full-blown, joy-filled, 3-D experience of strong masculine friendship with the men God has placed around you.

Walking free from the scars of our past is an ongoing process. Just as physical therapy can restore function to an injured limb, you can do some "emotional therapy" to overcome the disabilities caused by your wounds and scars. Here are a few ideas:

- Recognize painful areas when they arise. Ask yourself, "What areas do I continually remain sensitive to?" "Do I give in to sinful habits when those hurts resurface?"

- When you identify these issues, surrender them to the Lord. Ask for his help to respond in a healthier way the next time you're tempted. God knows the depth of your emotions—that sometimes a hurt has cut so deep that when you think about it, it's like a dry riverbed becoming a raging torrent when the floods come. Ask God to help you rechannel the flood of emotion that comes when those wounded areas are triggered.

- Share these tender areas and your decision to walk in a healthier way with a good friend who can pray for you and help you remain accountable for your decisions.

■ Receiving and Imparting the Blessing

Here's a question: Have you received your father's blessing? Has anyone physically put his hands on you and spoken blessing, affirmation, and identity into and over your life? If not, join the club. Few of us have. This biblical practice has become a lost art in the church today. The Jewish culture continues to model what we should value as a society. On their thirteenth birthdays, young men and women are celebrated into adulthood as their families and members of their synagogues surround them, recognize God's call on their lives and commit to walk with them to see that destiny fulfilled. What a powerful demonstration and initiation into adulthood!

Thankfully, God is restoring a similar practice to his church today—several books deal with the subject of imparting a father's blessing to our sons and daughters. You may be wondering how this issue is related to masculine friendship. Simply put, it's related in every way. We need friends who serve as "Jesus with skin on" to help us walk out the issues of life. It's the men around us who make us the husbands, fathers, and friends we're created to be as they speak encouragement, direction, correction, and affirmation into our lives.

I've had a number of men in my life who weren't ashamed to do this for me on a regular basis. Men like my friend Rick. He's a hulk of a man—a PE coach, fitness instructor, bodybuilder, and friend of mine for several years. Rick's arms are as big as my thighs. He's the kind of guy that warms up on two-hundred pounds more than your best bench press! Men notice and admire Rick's strength. Let me tell you what I admire most about him. Although we live in separate cities, whenever we see each other, Rick grabs me around the chest and squeezes me like a boa constrictor, literally lifting me off my feet. I love every minute of it (especially when I can breathe again)! He's a strong man who's not afraid to be close both physically and emotionally to other men. Rick and I can talk openly about anything going on in our lives. More than his bear hug embraces, Rick gives me something each time we meet. He imparts blessing. I thank God for such men who've taught me that any man is only half a man without another man beside him.

Sometimes women don't understand this dynamic about the men in their lives. They ask, "Are you saying that my husband's relationship with his buddies is more important than I am?" No, that's not what I mean. Strong male friendships could never compete with the oneness I share with my wife. But strong masculine friendship is like exercise. A man can live without it, but it will negatively affect his quality and length of life. Deep relationships with my male friends make me a better husband to my wife, a stronger father to my children, and a more devoted follower of Christ.

The point is that the absence of such relationships breeds hollow men. Proverbs 27:17 says, "As iron sharpens iron, so one man sharpens another." When I speak about this to men's groups, I say, "Your wife can't sharpen you! She can gnaw on you pretty good, but she can't sharpen you!" It takes other men to make you the husband, father, and friend you long to be. That's their job. Don't deny them the privilege. Receiving the affirmation, sharpening, and blessing of other men in your life isn't a sign of weakness. On the contrary, it's standard conduct for true warriors, and we'll be caught dead in battle without it.

According to Gary Smalley's and John Trent's classic book *The Blessing*, five basic elements[2] should be involved as you bless the people around you:

- *Meaningful touch.* Kneel down and place your hands on the person being blessed in an appropriate way. A hand on the shoulder or head communicates your love and approval.

- *Spoken word.* Verbalize the blessing. In a large gathering, you may want to use a microphone and record what is said as a reminder to the person being blessed. It can also be helpful to write ahead of time what you want to say.

- *Attach high value.* Speak about the character qualities and traits you see in that person as being unique gifts and talents from God. You can also communicate value by giving a gift. In my son's blessing ceremony, I gave him a family signet ring as a token of the high value we place on him.

- *Foresee a special future.* As God gives insight, pray for the life course of the person being blessed. Agree with what you see happening in his life and affirm the unique calling and gifting you recognize.

- *Commit to being part of that future.* Make sure the person being blessed knows that you're committing to help him walk out the calling of God by praying for him, giving counsel and direction he may need, and being his chief encourager along the way.

Of course, being able to do these things in your men's ministry means that you've spent some significant time getting to know the man you're blessing. But it's worth it. Receiving and imparting these significant values to others have been some of the most life changing and healing moments in my life.

■ Practicing See-Through Christianity

Another inescapable virtue of true masculine friendship is the issue of transparency. This can be tough for men because most our lives we've learned that real men should never be vulnerable or transparent. Many of us learned that from our culture, and had it reinforced in our churches. When I became a pastor, I was counseled that I shouldn't attempt to make close friends within my church.

It's pretty easy to understand why men don't want to be transparent and vulnerable. Most of us have been burned one time or another—after sharing something at a heart level only to later be betrayed. However, trying to live a stoic and internalized existence just sets men up for failure.

The trouble is, with few examples to follow, we don't really know what transparent living looks like. Fortunately Scripture contains several examples of men who modeled this healthier way of living, who demonstrated the need to have at least one male friend who knew what was going on with them. Let's take a peek behind the scenes on the lives of two men who typify God's pattern for transparency in man-to-man relationships. I'm referring, of course, to the two warrior friends David and Jonathan.

The curtain rises on David and Jonathan's friendship after David slew Goliath. Scripture records, "Jonathan became one in spirit with David, and he loved him as himself" (1 Samuel 18:1). What a great picture of biblical relationship—two warriors, knit together in spirit, unselfishly. Their deep friendship certainly wasn't a sign of weakness, as it might be seen if they were around in our culture. Let's not forget who David was: a fearless hunter, a giant killer! In 1 Samuel 16:18, it is said of David: "He is a brave man and a warrior." Yet David was also a man who recognized a strength deeper than that of his biceps—strong friendship.

The next exchange between the two friends is a clear indicator of how deep that bond went. 1 Samuel 18:3 says, "And Jonathan made a covenant with David because he loved him as himself." There's that phrase again. Do you have another man in your life you could say that about? Do you have a friend who you could tell anything to without it changing the way he looks at you? We need friends like that.

The commitment between Jonathan and David was so deep that they sealed it in the form of a covenant. In biblical days, covenant wasn't something people took lightly. *Covenant* implies an alliance, treaty, or league formed between individuals. David and Jonathan formed a holy bond of friendship. Fortunately we have some other illustrations of covenant in the Old Testament: The rainbow was a sign of God's covenant with Noah; the sacrificing of an animal on an altar was Israel's pledge of fidelity to God and a means to atone for sin; and the practice of circumcision was a pledge of consecration that "marked" a man, setting him apart for God.

We don't hear much about covenant these days. Of course, we live in a society where marriage vows are easily abandoned, and people often walk away from other relationships rather than walking through differences and difficulties together. It's no wonder that the concept of covenant is foreign to us. Paul addresses this lack of care and willingness to stick with and by one another in Galatians 5:14-15: "For the whole Law is fulfilled in one word, in the statement, 'You shall love your neighbor as yourself.' But if you bite and devour one another, take care that you are not consumed by one another."

In pre-marital counseling we tell couples, if you go into marriage believing that divorce is an option, you're likely to take it when, rather than if, the pressure of life gets turned up a notch or two. Relationships that go beyond casual acquaintances require this same kind of commitment. David and Jonathan weren't ashamed to make that kind of commitment to one another, and neither should we as brothers in Christ.

Of course, it's idealistic to think that there will never be times when two individuals have to part company over a particular issue. Even the Apostle Paul had his flap with Barnabas. But even in those times, there's a proper way to handle the situation that honors both the relationship and the other person. (More on this later.) A church populated by men committed to walking together through whatever difficulties come along couldn't build an auditorium big enough to hold the people who'd be drawn to a place where they could have that kind of relationship.

This relational dynamic doesn't happen most effectively in an arena of fifty thousand guys or even in a large group at your church. Instead, it happens when two or three men get together on a regular basis to share life. That's why men enjoy sitting in bars for hours swapping "manly stories" or patting teammates on the rear after a successful punt return on the football field (try doing *that* at your next men's meeting)! Of course, those examples are hollow representations of the real relational fiber that connects men who truly share their hearts and lives with each other.

I've stayed up all night with guys discussing deep heart issues—a recent breakup with a girlfriend, fears and frustrations about the future, the heartache of a parent's divorce. It saddens me that these conversations aren't more common among Christian men. Instead, we often feel compelled to hide our weaknesses, and we live in isolation and shame. How much tragedy could be avoided if men were afforded the luxury of just being honest with one another. Instead, we feel pressured to stand as Lone Ranger "Super Christian Studs," covering up what's really going on inside, scared to death someone will find out.

Without transparent relationships life is a frustrating charade. Genuine transparency can only be achieved in an atmosphere of trust, and trust is forged in the fires of covenant.

Of course, it's pretty hard to create an atmosphere of trust amid the strong spirit of competitiveness among men in the church today. Only when we cease viewing each other as competitors and, instead, treat one another as co-laborers, will we experience the blessing of Psalm 133: "Behold, how good and pleasant it is when brothers dwell in unity" (Revised Standard Version).

Being transparent and authentic doesn't come naturally for most men. Or even getting together with other guys—especially to work on relationships—doesn't come that naturally either. In your ministry to men, you'll have to start slow and help men develop relationships gradually. But making the effort is worth it!

A couple of suggestions for getting started:

- Look for common interest areas. Sporting activities, movies, and service projects are safe places where relationships can begin to form among men. Two or three guys painting a widow's house on a Saturday will probably do more to build relationship among them than they'd ever find during many weeks of sharing burnt pancakes!

- Invite a friend to breakfast. Let the conversation guide you into areas where you have common interests. If you do this regularly, you'll soon find a man just like you who is looking for an invitation to open his heart. Imagine if all the men on your leadership team would open up to just one other guy in this way. Now that would be a ministry to men!

■ Caring Enough to Confront

Because I grew up in an alcoholic and abusive home, for a long time I had a skewed perspective of confrontation. When I was a kid, confrontation usually meant that someone got physically hurt.

Eventually I came to understand and appreciate the value of healthy and God-honoring confrontation, which should be a normal part of the natural flow of any relationship. Whether between husband and wife, parent and child, or brothers in Christ, confrontation is normal and necessary. It still isn't particularly pleasant—and I'd be leery of anyone who enjoys the act of confrontation. But I've learned that it can be a sign of a deep caring for those we love and those who love us.

To understand what healthy confrontation looks like in our relationships, it helps to look at its opposite: criticism. Criticism is nothing more than the luxury of noninvolvement. In other words, if you're not committed relationally to someone, you allow yourself the privileged position of standing back with arms folded, critiquing his every move. Criticism simply causes heartache and a broken spirit. If you're truly committed to someone's success, you'll go beyond simply bringing up an issue; you'll roll up your sleeves and volunteer to pitch in and help resolve the situation. Imagine if that were the dominant attitude in churches today!

Again, an episode in David's life demonstrates this principle. You'll recall that David had taken a fancy to a certain bathing beauty who happened to be someone else's wife. Blinded by his own lust, the king conveniently arranged for the husband's untimely death on the battlefield. The prophet Nathan stepped into this sad situation as God's mouthpiece to confront David. Matthew Henry, in his commentary on the story in 2 Samuel 12, says that we see Nathan's true heart in this act of friendship. "Nathan was obedient to the heavenly vision, and went on God's errand to David. He did not say, 'David has sinned, I will not come near him.' *No—count him not an enemy, but admonish him as a brother.*" Paul gives much the same instruction in 2 Thessalonians 3:15, saying that if we catch someone in sin, we should "not regard him as an enemy, but warn him as a brother."

Of course, how we receive confrontation is also critical in the equation. Are you open to the Lord using another man to expose your shortcomings? In the context of relationship, we need to have tender, teachable hearts that are open to hearing things we don't necessarily want to acknowledge before others.

Face it, you can tell the difference between someone who is simply criticizing you and someone who God is using to confront you and hold you accountable for your words, actions, and attitudes. Oh, for a more tender heart toward the Spirit's conviction and for the courage to respond in brokenness and humility when God uses another man to bring about healing. "Faithful are the wounds of a friend, but deceitful are the kisses of an enemy" (Proverbs 27:6, New American Standard Bible). What an awesome verse! Wouldn't you rather be wounded by the gentle and humble confrontations of a friend than kissed by a flattering enemy? Deep friendship requires that we commit to confronting our brother in the right spirit when necessary. And it requires that we quickly acknowledge our own sin and repent when we're confronted.

No one enjoys (or certainly, no one should enjoy) the process of confronting others or being confronted. But it's a necessary and healthy part of relationships among Christian men. These guidelines can help make confrontation slightly easier to do:

- *Pray!* Ask God to confirm for you clearly that you have a deep enough relationship with the man to gently confront him.

- *Pray more.* This time, ask God to confirm for you that you're seeing your friend's actions clearly—that he's really doing something he needs to be confronted about.

- *Pray still more.* Once God has confirmed the above for you, pray that his grace will soften the heart of the man you're confronting so that you're really heard.

- *Set a specific time and place to meet.* Consider a public place like a restaurant. Your conversation is more likely to be controlled, and your friend will be less likely to overreact emotionally.

- *Use the biblical model found in Matthew 18:15-17.* Go to the man privately and share your concerns. If your friend doesn't respond to you, take along another guy or two you both respect. If that doesn't work, bring the leaders of your church into the situation to help navigate the process to a loving conclusion.

- *Stay humble in your attempt to bring correction.* Don't be guilty of pointing out the speck in your brother's eye while ignoring the log in your own. Humility is the key that can open even the hardest heart.

■ Making Time to Connect

When you desire to help the men in your church develop deeper relationships with each other, one thing affects everything else you'll do. That one thing is time. Without an intentional commitment to invest whatever it takes to call men into deeper relationships with one another and with God, our best programs, events, activities, and overall ministry for men will be short lived and not matter much in the light of eternity. As someone has said, "I don't fear failure as much as I do succeeding at something that doesn't matter."

Succeeding in helping men develop healthy and valued relationships (and having those kinds of relationships ourselves) means that we need to get serious about where and how we invest our time. Just as a good marriage takes work to prevent the relational atrophy that naturally occurs without continued attention and maintenance, the same is true in our relationships with other guys. We'll only get close as we become willing to invest the time it takes to go beyond simply being casual acquaintances. If we're committed to developing deep, satisfying, and life-giving relationships with other Christian men, it will require an intentional process to keep those connections active and growing.

If we don't make this a priority, we're liable to find ourselves relationally stranded and friendless.

To keep our relationships connected and growing, we need to make some important decisions about how we use the time we've been given. Look at it from a different perspective: If every waking minute of your life was a dollar that you could spend on whatever you wanted, each day you'd have more than a thousand bucks to do with as you please. (You'd technically have $1,440, but you'd probably want to invest at least $440 a day on sleep or no one would want to be your friend!) You choose how you spend the thousand each day, but the catch is that once you spend it, it's *gone*.

Someone has said the best things to invest your life in are the things that will outlast it. People certainly fit that category. So how will you spend your time? On the things that will outlast it? If investing in deeper relationships with other men is truly important to you, it will cost you something. Like me, I know you want to give your life to the things that matter most. Rick Warren says it like this: "Often we act as if relationships are something to be squeezed into our schedule. We talk about finding time for our children, or making time for people in our lives. That gives the impression that relationships are just a part of our lives along with many other tasks. But God says relationships are what life is all about."[3]

Do you want to get to the end of your life and say, "I never had any friends." How do you develop relationships? Intentionally. On purpose. It's like those "God billboards" you may have seen that, in stark black and white graphics, grab the attention of passing motorists with a God-thought. One of my favorites is, "That 'Love your neighbor as yourself' thing...I *meant* that." This mandate was given as a command, not as an option. To enjoy deep masculine friendships requires that we don the armor and go to battle with the beast called "time."

The Final Word

When it comes to developing relationships among men, there's certainly no easy answer—no "just add water" instant solution. You can't line up guys against the wall of your church, point a gun at them, and demand that they relate!

Yet men are hungry for *relationships*—not more things to do. This means that no matter what activities you plan for the men's ministry in your church, *building relationships* must be the ultimate purpose that you aim for. Yes, you need to create opportunities to get together. But strong friendships will never form by just getting guys together in the same room. *Life* must be present for relationships to form—and that takes work!

It won't be an easy task. It will take an immense amount of prayer, forethought, and strategic planning. You'll get discouraged, tired, worn out. In fact, the enemy must know the untapped power of men united in strong relationships—otherwise he wouldn't work so hard at discouraging us from doing it.

Essentially, we've been focusing on three basic truths about what it takes to draw men into closer relationships:

1. Believing that deep, committed friendships are absolutely vital in the process of equipping men to be the leaders God calls them to be—in their homes, with their families, in their churches, and beyond.

2. Submitting the wounds of our hearts to the Healer so we can freely pursue authentic relationships with others.

3. Intentionally inviting men to join us in recovering the lost strength of male friendship.

Some of the best advice I've ever received about men's ministry came during a moment of total desperation. I'd just spent considerable time, energy, and money to research and purchase a respected organization's latest tapes and books, hoping that these materials would be "the answer" to reaching men. But when I couldn't figure out what to do or even where to start with the $140 kit I'd bought, I called the organization and expressed my frustration. The man who answered the phone understood. His wise counsel was simple, yet profound. He said, "Find two other guys, rip out the pages that apply to you, and go deep."

That's really what it boils down to. This book is filled with dozens of great ideas from men who know what they're talking about. But ideas are just "one more thing to do" unless they're birthed in an atmosphere of relationship. The ideas must be applied in the laboratory of day-to-day living where lasting friendships are forged in the fires of adversity. This process must serve as the backbone of your ministry to men. This is the example Jesus showed us. He took a few men and "went deep." That model of ministry to men has radically changed the world, and it's unlikely that we can improve much on the original concept.

Tim Doyle

Tim Doyle is director of Joseph Resource Group, a ministry serving and connecting churches and church leaders in the Midwest. He and his wife, Krista, are the parents of two sons.

Visit his Web site at: www.JRGroup.org.

Endnotes

1. See the National Fatherhood Initiative, "Top Ten Father Facts" at: www.fatherhood.org/fatherfacts/topten.htm

2. Gary Smalley and John Trent, *The Blessing* (New York: Pocket Books, 1986), 27.

3. See Rick Warren's "Saddleback Sayings" at: www.pastors.com.

BIBLE STUDIES: INTO THE WORD AND EACH OTHER'S LIVES

I t's said that our society views men as self-reliant, unable to feel or express emotion, unconcerned about fellowship, using people but loving things, primarily competitive, and too macho. If this is the case, then you're taking an important step toward changing that view.

You probably see many men week to week at your church who are longing for relationship. They desire to meet regularly with a small group of other men where they can safely reveal their problems and receive support to overcome them. A men's small group can provide tremendous encouragement as men discover that they're not alone with their destructive relational patterns or "secret sins." The following studies for men—which you can copy and distribute to the men in your group—emphasize this kind of self-exploration and candid sharing.

What happens to men who *don't* find a group where they can openly share their struggles and build deeper relationships? Often, they'll bog down in their spiritual journeys in one of two ways.

1. Some men continue *trying to control their circumstances*. You'll see this in the guy who says, "I believe I *should* be joyful; I *should* feel fulfilled. But I never seem to reach it. I try and try, but something always goes wrong." When faced with dissatisfaction in life, he tries to overcome it by trying to force happiness. Unfortunately it never works.

2. Other men keep *trying to "act the part."* This is almost the opposite approach. You'll see this tendency in the guy who tries to act as if things really are working out great all the time. He's not content with savoring the blessings and joys God sprinkles into his years, so he pretends to experience unbroken daily bliss. In effect, he begins to fake his faith, wearing the mask of continual victory. Of course that doesn't work for long either.

Unfortunately not many of us have embraced the more authentic Christian approach to life: *learning to embrace the pain and struggle of life.* This isn't an easy route to take. But it's the most honest. It brings us down to a basic reality—that everything we are and have is a product of the pure, unconditional grace of God.

Here's the key point: This authentic approach to Christian living *can't be done in a vacuum.* It requires fellowship, mutual encouragement, and ongoing accountability as men meet together to discuss their successes and failures, and the worries, fears, and concerns they need to pray about. Only in these authentic relationships can we help each other live for God and grow in our faith.

How to Use These Studies

The following Bible studies are for men who desire to meet together to share their lives with one another. Your group might meet in a conference room or restaurant at lunchtime, at a coffee shop for an early morning breakfast, or in a guy's home in the evening after dinner.

These sessions work especially well in groups of three to ten men. Make sure each guy has a copy of the study. The same leader can facilitate the discussion each week, or your group can use rotating leadership. While the studies work best if participants have read the material before you meet, the studies are short enough to skim or even read aloud during the group meeting. The study format allows you to simply "lay out material" for discussion. The guys in your group will realize this and feel free to let their discussions move into their particular areas of concern.

Preparing to Lead a Group Session

Whether you lead each study or take turns, your job is to act as a discussion facilitator not a teacher. Before the session, spend some time thinking about how the readings relate to your own spiritual growth journey. *Answer the three questions below, and you'll have all the material you need for generating discussion* as others will feel free to contribute their own insights, comments, and questions in response. Of course you may also draw upon the "For Further Discussion" section, as your session time permits.

1. What experience in my own life confirms (or disputes) the material I've read?

2. What themes or statements stood out to me as most important, significant, or controversial?

3. What questions, comments, insights, or personal applications flow from this material?

Getting a Handle on the Format

Each study contains the following items. Your group can focus on any or all of the story sections that relate to their experiences. The goal is personal application, in the context of group accountability, for the purpose of spiritual growth and deepening relationships.

■ Session Starter

You might call this an icebreaker or a warm-up. The idea is to ease your group into the study and get the guys talking to each other.

■ One Man's Story

This brief vignette offers the experience of one man with the study's topic. It's a personal "how-I-experience-this-issue" story, intended to put the topic into the context of everyday life.

■ God Enters the Story

This section includes Scripture passages related to the topic, printed as part of the study so no one feels left out because he's unfamiliar with looking up passages in the Bible. Your group may focus heavily on these verses or you might simply let the Scripture serve as a boundary for your discussion. Often our own stories (the way we actually live) clash with God's story (the call to deeper commitment and holiness). This tension makes for excellent discussion: How can God's story become, to a greater degree, the story of our own Christian growth?

■ The Story in Quotes

These brief statements are intended to add spice to your discussion. Some are profound insights, others are controversial thought starters. Some of your group members may agree with the statements, others may disagree.

■ Can You Relate?

For this part of your study—which will probably consume most of your time together as a group—you'll focus on the following four questions each week:

1. Which one of the three story sections in this study did you connect with most? Why?

2. As you read the story sections, did any of your own stories or experiences come to mind?

3. What other insights came to you? What questions did this study raise in your mind? Do you have any personal application you'd like to tell the group about?

4. What else would you like to say about this study's topic?

The leader uses these questions to make up the basic "plan" of the session time. Your group might spend most of its time responding to these questions. But if you have extra time, you can also go through the "For Further Discussion" questions.

■ Suggestions for the Week Ahead

These suggestions are meant to provide practical life responses related to the study's main topic. Group members can choose the suggestions that will help them take the first steps toward change.

■ Prayer Moments

Each week allow time for guys in your group to share specific prayer requests. Then choose one of the following approaches and spend time praying as a group. Varying the approach will help group members pray in ways that are comfortable for them.

- One volunteer prays, covering the group's requests, issues, and concerns.
- Each person prays for the man seated to his right.
- Pray sentence prayers, designating someone to start and to close.
- Focus on one key concern of the group or a group member; everyone prays about that concern as each feels led.
- Spend some moments in silent prayer.
- Assign specific requests to people before going into your prayer time.
- Lay hands on one man who expresses need, and focus on his prayer request.
- Other methods: _____

_____

You might want to keep a journal or some other record of your prayers, listing dates when you prayed and noting answers to prayer. You can photocopy the "Prayer Record" on page 166 to distribute to group members. Seeing God work in your lives will deepen your relationships with each other and with him.

So...ready to begin? Call the men, set a time and a place for your weekly meetings, and get started!

Gary Wilde

Gary Wilde has worked as a freelance editor for fifteen years. He developed the *Encouragers for Men* series and is author of *Mantras, Menorahs, and Minarets: Encountering Other Faiths*. A former pastor, he's editor of the devotional magazine The Quiet Hour and co-author of *Receiving Love*. His hobbies include singing in a barbershop quartet and snorkling in Florida's springs.

Uniting Through Shared Experience

■ Session Starter

If your group is new and the men don't know each other, start with this icebreaker activity. Ask each person to form a pair with someone he knows the least. Give each pair a sheet of paper and a pencil. State that the pairs will have exactly 4½ minutes (use a timer, if possible) to create as long a list as they can of things they have in common. All the items on their lists should relate to any of these three topics:

1. Childhood background

2. Past or present work

3. Recreation or hobbies

At the end of the time limit, ask pairs to briefly share with the whole group what they have in common.

Make your transition to the session theme by pointing out that in this session, you'll be exploring together the importance of shared experience for men who hope to deepen their relationships.

■ One Man's Story

We pulled our canoes onto the beach of a little island in the middle of central Florida's St. John's River. Dale, Calvin, Steve, and I—four young men from Downey Community Church on a weekend adventure—spent the rest of the day setting up our camp, looking for dry wood, and scouting around the place until evening. Around dusk we stumbled upon something scary. I found it—a huge skinned alligator lying in the midst of a crop of tall palmetto bushes. The eyes were still in the gator's head, and it had its tail and claws, but the rest of its body had been mutilated into a massive strip of slick, gray strands of flesh. It lay there stinking in the hot sun, the flies buzzing.

With a lump in my throat, I ran back and told the group. We all returned to survey the scene and then crept back to our camp wondering: *Who would do this—some sort of knife-toting outlaws? Where are they now? And exactly how far are we from civilization?*

It got dark too soon. We sat mostly silent around our campfire. But later as we tried to fall asleep in the tent—a flimsy canvas shelter against ruthless poachers—we began to talk. I can't remember much of the conversation, but I know I began to feel closer to these guys than I ever had before. Part of it was the fear of what might be lurking outside our tent! We'd need each other for protection. But the experience of seeing the alligator had brought us together, as well. We'd all seen it. We'd all been shocked by it. Only the four of us knew what it looked like, and we had a story to tell that no one else would ever experience firsthand.

I know some guys who would never even consider coming to a group to "talk about life." But I know they've had experiences of camaraderie, of bonding with other guys. And I'm tempted to believe that just being together—working or playing or accomplishing a goal—has something to do with deepening relationships. At least it's a starting point.

—Gary Wilde

■ God Enters the Story

Mary Magdalene went to the disciples with the news: "I have seen the Lord!"

On the evening of that first day of the week, when the disciples were together, with the doors locked for fear of the Jews, Jesus came and stood among them and said, "Peace be with you!" After he said this, he showed them his hands and side. The disciples were overjoyed when they saw the Lord.

—John 20:18-20

That which was from the beginning, which we have heard, which we have seen with our eyes, which we have looked at and our hands have touched—this we proclaim concerning the Word of life. The life appeared; we have seen it and testify to it, and we proclaim to you the eternal life, which was with the Father and has appeared to us. We proclaim to you what we have seen and heard, so that you also may have fellowship with us. And our fellowship is with the Father and with his Son, Jesus Christ. We write this to make our joy complete.

—1 John 1:1-4

■ The Story in Quotes

"It has been said that true friendship begins only when people share a common memory and can say to each other, 'Do you remember?' Each of us [Christian disciples] is one of a great fellowship of people who share a common experience and a common memory of their Lord."

—William Barclay, *The Daily Study Bible*

"Though activities do not guarantee solid relationships, men seem to need activities more than women do to get to know one another better...For most men, therefore, coming together in a small group to discuss life in general and their life in particular is an uncomfortable experience."

—Geoff Gorsuch with Dan Schaffer
Brothers! Calling Men Into Vital Relationships

■ Can You Relate?

As a group, discuss these questions:

1. Which one of the three story sections in this study did you connect with most? Why?

2. As you read the story sections, did any of your own stories or experiences come to mind?

3. What other insights came to you? What questions did this study raise in your mind? Do you have any personal application you'd like to tell the group about?

4. What else would you like to say about this study's topic?

■ For Further Discussion

• When does fear tend to make you more talkative? less talkative?

• Is being in a men's small group comfortable or uncomfortable for you? What things help you to feel more at ease in a group?

• Do you agree that "men seem to need activities more than women" in order to get to know each other? Explain, and give a personal example, if you can.

• How do you think the disciples felt when they gathered together after Jesus had left them? (See Acts 1:9-14.)

• Why was the experience of hearing, seeing, and touching Jesus so important to the Apostle John? How did he relate this experience to Christian relationships?

• In your opinion, how is any shared experience like and unlike the shared experience of new life in Christ? Describe the similarities and differences of "male bonding" and the unique nature of Christian relationship.

• What experiences can your group members recall sharing with other groups of guys? What things could this group do together to deepen your relationships?

■ Prayer Moments

Ask for prayer requests, and close with prayer. (*Leader:* See page 130 for a list of various approaches to group prayer.)

■ Suggestion for the Week Ahead

During a quiet time this week, list some recreational activities you enjoy. On the opposite side of the paper, list names of men you'd like to know better—either men in your group or acquaintances outside the group. Consider reaching out to establish or deepen a friendship with one of these guys by inviting him to join you for a recreational activity.

Committing to Listening

■ Session Starter

As members of your group arrive, hand each of them a sheet of construction paper with yarn attached to the top corners. The paper should hang at chest level when it's put around the neck. Ask each person to write on the paper one word, in large letters, that states what he does for a living—for example, "Carpenter."

When each guy is wearing his occupation-sign necklace, state that during this study, whenever anyone speaks to someone else, he must use the occupation-word of the other person in each sentence.

After you've let some informal conversation using this rule go on for two minutes, stop everything. Take a moment to debrief by asking for comments about how it felt to be identified solely by an occupation label. Ask if anyone feels that way in real life. Then note that today's study will focus on committing to a form of listening that goes beyond labeling others.

■ One Man's Story

I know a guy, I'll call him Ernie, who has an irritating relational habit. I don't see Ernie all that much, and maybe that's the reason this problem continues. But every time I run into Ernie, he greets me with the same question about a part of my work life that I once shared with him.

This seems to be Ernie's way of dealing with my "case." This one small piece of information about me has apparently, for Ernie, become the whole of me. So in spite of his warm handshake, I feel as though he's closing me off.

I know I've told Ernie more about myself over the years than this one small tidbit. But I've wondered if I'll ever want to go much deeper in our relationship because I always have the sense that Ernie just isn't listening.

Unfortunately this experience isn't confined to Ernie and me. In fact, it characterizes what often takes place between other guys and me at church following our weekly service. We all greet one another and pick up with the same old small talk. I realize that I have unintentionally pigeonholed most of those guys by mentally filing away their "stories" under one label. For example, there's the guy who got a promotion last year—or was it the year before? There's the couple with a son in medical school. And there's a young man who coaches at the high school. When I see these people at church, it's as if I'm talking to a promotion, a scalpel, and a football rather than to individuals involved with me in the adventure of spiritual growth.

So I come to my men's group—a gathering of my Christian brothers—and hope each week it will be different. I don't want to see worn-out labels when I look at the warm people in my group. I want to learn to hear with my heart about what's happening in their lives now and to listen with my feelings for their feelings. The concerns and struggles of these guys are my issues too. I can learn from them, and our time together is too precious for me to treat it as mere conversational white noise.

In short, I have a chance to be a part of ever-deepening relationships with a few other guys. Lord, help me not to close it off by failing to listen with all my heart.

—Gary Wilde

■ God Enters the Story

You, [Timothy], know all about my teaching, my way of life, my purpose, faith, patience, love, endurance, persecutions, sufferings—what kinds of things happened to me in Antioch, Iconium and Lystra, the persecutions I endured.

—2 Timothy 3:10-11

Speaking the truth in love, we will in all things grow up into him who is the Head, that is, Christ. From him the whole body, joined and held together by every supporting ligament, grows and builds itself up in love, as each part does its work…Therefore each of you must put off falsehood and speak truthfully to his neighbor, for we are all members of one body.

—Ephesians 4:15-16, 25

■ The Story in Quotes

"Guys don't talk to each other. We paw up dirt, we bang antlers, sometimes we graze side by side, but we seldom talk. [There are many] ancient guy myths, but the biggest myth of all is that men can open up to each other and share their secrets."

—Garrison Keillor, *The Book of Guys*

"The person who tells the story bestows a gift on the listener. The person who attends and appreciatively receives bestows a gift on the teller…There is probably no service we can render other persons quite as great or important as to be listener and receiver."

—Thomas N. Hart, *The Art of Christian Listening*

■ Can You Relate?

As a group, discuss these questions:

1. Which one of the three story sections in this study did you connect with most? Why?

2. As you read the story sections, did any of your own stories or experiences come to mind?

3. What other insights came to you? What questions did this study raise in

your mind? Do you have any personal application you'd like to tell the group about?

4. What else would you like to say about this study's topic?

■ For Further Discussion

• Do you agree with Garrison Keillor that guys "graze side by side" but seldom talk? Explain.

• What would it mean for you to listen with your feelings for another man's feelings? If possible, give an example.

• According to the Apostle Paul, Timothy knew all about him. How do you think this happened? Do you have any friends that close?

• How does "speaking the truth" to one another help improve our listening skills? How would you rate the listening skills in your group? Can you give an example of how these skills have operated successfully?

• How is telling your story a "gift" to another guy? How is attentive listening a gift?

• When was the last time you gave or received this gift of listening—you truly listened, or you really felt listened to? How did that experience affect you?

■ Prayer Moments

Ask for prayer requests, and close with prayer. (**Leader:** See page 130 for a list of various approaches to group prayer.)

■ Suggestion for the Week Ahead

Think through some of the "surface" interactions you've had with men during the last couple of weeks or months. Then focus on this common situation: You know a man at church, work, or in your neighborhood who you see frequently. Perhaps you converse in passing, but you've never really taken the time to have a more extended conversation.

The next time you see him, stop whatever you're doing and go for a more significant interaction. You might say: "You know, we see each other all the time, and I've been thinking I'd like to get to know you better..." Make the first move, and begin a conversation. Determine to listen closely to the man's words, both for what his words *say* and for what they *mean*. Perhaps this will be a first step toward a new friendship.

Risking "Realness"

■ Session Starter

Ask the men in your group to bring photos of themselves from childhood to this session. Encourage each person to find a photo of himself at a very young age—even infancy, if possible. If they can't find pictures, they can bring objects from their childhood, such as toys, yearbooks, or awards. If anyone comes without a photo or an object, he can secretively write his childhood nickname on an index card. *Note*: Photos and objects should be brought in bags so that no one will know who the owners are.

Take the photos, objects, and nickname cards to another room. Using sticky notes, label the items with numbers. Return to the room with the items. Hand out paper and pencils, and invite the group members to make a numbered list, guessing which guy brought each photo or object or guessing who the nickname belongs to.

When everyone has a list, reveal the correct answers. As you go through the answer list, invite guys to tell why they guessed either correctly or incorrectly. Encourage each participant to share about the photo or object and tell how easy or tough it was to reveal this part of his life. Also invite guys to answer this question:

- How much or how little do you believe you've changed since that point in your life?

State that during this study you'll be exploring the importance of risking realness as you develop deeper relationships.

Option: Instead of asking men to bring something to the session, just use the nickname-on-the-index-card idea. Share together about how hard or easy it was to reveal a former nickname. Talk about how those childhood nicknames do or don't characterize each of you now.

■ One Man's Story

I suppose I was a bit of a bully at that point in my life—including the day I decided to make fun of Debbie at the pool. I was just a twelve-year-old kid, and I was calling her things I can't even remember. But I do remember how Debbie responded.

I can still see her walking over to my little pile of stuff—T-shirt, socks, and gym shoes—picking them up, marching over to the deep end of the pool, and ceremoniously dropping everything into the water. As everyone watched, my white socks floated away from one another like two dead, belly-up catfish. The shoes sank quickly. But the T-shirt ballooned out and hung just below the surface like a monstrous jellyfish.

I was crushed.

What could I do to regain a bit of my dignity? I stood on the diving board, and as giggles and guffaws rang in my ears, a red-hot tingling shot up into my face. The more I tried to control that swelling, dam-burst of a blush, the more I imagined myself a ripe, purple grape ready to explode. I wanted one thing more than anything else—to be anywhere but on that diving board.

Something changed inside the boy that day, in a way that still endures in the man. The next day in homeroom—where Debbie sat across from me, two rows over—I succumbed to a new form of self-consciousness I'd never known before. I was sure that kids were looking at me in ways they'd never looked at me before. And when Debbie really did turn to look at me, I had to decide in a split second what my response would be.

So I grinned as if to say, "You didn't hurt me, you know. In fact, no one has ever hurt me, and no one ever will."

I've heard that every child comes to a day when he exchanges his real self for his false self. In effect, he gives over his innocent childhood face for a mask, a flimsy caricature that hardens until it's ready for everyday use in the adult world. He chooses rigid protection over the risk of honest disclosure.

That day at the pool and the next day at school, I began to mold my new face.

—Gary Wilde

■ God Enters the Story

Then the eyes of both of them were opened, and they realized they were naked; so they sewed fig leaves together and made coverings for themselves.

Then the man and his wife heard the sound of the Lord God as he was walking in the garden in the cool of the day, and they hid from the Lord God among the trees of the garden. But the Lord God called to the man, "Where are you?"

He answered, "I heard you in the garden, and I was afraid because I was naked; so I hid."

And he said, "Who told you that you were naked?"
—Genesis 3:7-11a

O Lord, you have searched me and you know me.
—Psalm 139:1

Therefore, brothers, since we have confidence to enter the Most Holy Place by the blood of Jesus, by a new and living way opened for us through the curtain, that is, his body, and since we have a great priest over the house of God, let us draw near to God with a sincere heart in full assurance of

faith, having our hearts sprinkled to cleanse us from a guilty conscience and having our bodies washed with pure water.
—Hebrews 10:19-22

In this way, love is made complete among us so that we will have confidence on the day of judgment, because in this world we are like him. There is no fear in love. But perfect love drives out fear, because fear has to do with punishment. The one who fears is not made perfect in love.
—1 John 4:17-18

■ The Story in Quotes

"No man for any considerable period can wear one face to himself and another to the multitude, without finally getting bewildered as to which may be the true."
—Nathaniel Hawthorne

"I believe they talked of me, for they laughed consumedly."
—George Farquhar

■ Can You Relate?

As a group, discuss these questions:

1. Which one of the three story sections in this study did you connect with most? Why?

2. As you read the story sections, did any of your own stories or experiences come to mind?

3. What other insights came to you? What questions did this study raise in your mind? Do you have any personal application you'd like to tell the group about?

4. What else would you like to say about this study's topic?

■ For Further Discussion

• What defining moments can you recall from your childhood—events that have significantly influenced the kind of man you are today? (For example, it may have been a great blessing that came your way, a terrible blow, or a momentous decision.)

• Do you agree that there's a point in a person's life when he begins to wear a mask? Why or why not?

• How difficult is it for you to know your true self? Do you struggle to reveal that self to other men?

• In your opinion, what is the spiritual significance of Adam and Eve realizing they were naked? How would you compare their attempt to cover up with our desire to project a positive image of ourselves?

• What does it mean for you to "draw near to God with a sincere heart"?

• What do you think John meant by his statement that there is no fear in love? How have you seen this truth confirmed in human relationships?

• How does the fear of vulnerability lead to a desire to control? Give a practical example.

• Look again at the quote from George Farquhar. To what extent does our perception of what others are thinking affect our ability to be open and real? Can you give a personal example?

■ Prayer Moments

Ask for prayer requests, and close with prayer. (**Leader:** See page 130 for a list of various approaches to group prayer.)

■ Suggestion for the Week Ahead

During the week, take some time to think about one of your defining moments from childhood. Hold this event in your mind for a while, and let it crystallize in your memory so that you begin to feel just how powerful it was for you at the time.

After a few minutes, take a sheet of paper and create a drawing of a mask. Let this mask represent your "face"—your personality as an adult. On the mask draw eyes, ears, and mouth to represent the following:

Eyes: How I "see" the world today (generally optimistic or mostly pessimistic?)

Ears: What I "hear" when I sense God speaking to me (messages of blessing and grace or messages of condemnation and judgment?)

Mouth: What I "say" to others in relationships (am I open and real, genuine and encouraging, or fearful and closed up?)

Next to the eyes, ears, and mouth, write words from the phrases above that characterize you. Then think about these questions:

• What link do I draw between how I am today and what happened to me in the past—in my defining moments?

• Are any of these connections hard for me to face? Difficult to reveal to others? Why?

• Which connections should I keep to myself as a means of setting legitimate personal boundaries?

• Which might I risk revealing to other guys—with the hope that they'll open up to me—as a means of deepening our relationships?

Dreaming of the Future

■ Session Starter

Give each guy an index card and a pen. Say something like, "Think through your childhood and teenage years and even your college years. Make a list of some of the things you wanted to be when you grew up." If you get questions, explain that you're trying to get men to list the vocational dreams and goals they've had in the past. Now ask them to arrange their lists in chronological order to illustrate how their plans have changed over the years.

When everyone has a list, ask for the cards, shuffle them, and read them aloud as the group tries to guess whose card is whose. Once the group has guessed correctly or you reveal whose card you're reading, ask each guy to provide more detail about the "success" or "failure" of his vocational plans.

The connection to this study's theme: coping with frustrated dreams.

■ One Man's Story

I was to be the next Billy Graham—so I thought as a teenager. Amazingly, thirty years later, I learned that the guy working in the cubicle next to me also expected to be the future Billy Graham. I then wondered how many Billy Grahams-to-be grew up during the 1950s.

Later I matured. I thought I'd be a seminary professor. People told me so, and I even have a Ph.D. Three guys from my graduating class are presidents of Christian colleges or seminaries. Two of the three once recommended me for honors or positions I never received. And the third—well, no one in our class would have ever picked him as the president of…well, I won't name the school. Now that I've passed the half-century mark, I'm still wondering what I'll be when I grow up!

My dreams didn't include sitting at a desk evaluating oh-so-thrilling nursery level Sunday school curriculum. When midlife crisis got me depressed, a counselor told me that I needed to come to terms with life's three A's: accept, adapt, or alter.

Accept life. Just as it is. Just as I am. Who am I to say to the divine Potter "Why am I where I am?" I have a great wife. I have wonderful friends. I have ministry opportunities. Jesus spent ten-elevenths of his life not doing "ministry."

Adapt. If one of my dreams was to be a seminary professor, why can't I perform that same role whenever God gives me people to lead and teach? My dream can be modified to fit my personal circumstances.

Alter. Perhaps I'm too laid back about achieving my aims. Do I need to send out more résumés? Do I expect God to just drop my dream job in my lap, or shall I say with Paul, "I labor, struggling with all his energy"?

An old song says, "I know not what the future holds, but I know who holds the future." Can I learn to say with Paul, "I have learned the secret of being content in any and every situation"?

—Jim Townsend

God Enters the Story

Now this is what the Lord Almighty says: "Give careful thought to your ways. You have planted much, but have harvested little. You eat, but never have enough. You drink, but never have your fill. You put on clothes, but are not warm. You earn wages, only to put them in a purse with holes in it."

This is what the Lord Almighty says: "Give careful thought to your ways. Go up into the mountains and bring down timber and build the house, so that I may take pleasure in it and be honored," says the Lord. "You expected much, but see, it turned out to be little. What you brought home, I blew away. Why?" declares the Lord Almighty. "Because of my house, which remains a ruin, while each of you is busy with his own house. Therefore, because of you the heavens have withheld their dew and the earth its crops. I called for a drought on the fields and the mountains, on the grain, the new wine, the oil and whatever the ground produces, on men and cattle, and on the labor of your hands."

—Haggai 1:5-11

"For I know the plans I have for you," declares the Lord, "plans to prosper you and not to harm you, plans to give you hope and a future."

—Jeremiah 29:11

But seek first his kingdom and his righteousness, and all these things will be given to you as well.

—Matthew 6:33

The Story in Quotes

"Ever reach a point in your life where you say, 'This is the best I'm ever going to look, ever going to feel, ever going to do…and it ain't that great'?"

—Billy Crystal, as Mitch, in the movie *City Slickers*

"Among all my patients in the second half of life—that is to say over thirty-five—there has not been one whose problem in the last resort was not that of finding a religious outlook on life."

—Carl Jung

"Being religious means asking passionately the question of the meaning of our existence and being willing to receive answers, even if the answers hurt."

—Paul Tillich

■ Can You Relate?

As a group, discuss these questions:

1. Which one of the three story sections in this study did you connect with most? Why?

2. As you read the story sections, did any of your own stories or experiences come to mind?

3. What other insights came to you? What questions did this study raise in your mind? Do you have any personal application you'd like to tell the group about?

4. What else would you like to say about this study's topic?

■ For Further Discussion

- Which of the following sentences comes closest to describing you: (1) All my dreams are coming to pass, or (2) my dreams never seem to work out. If neither sentence describes you, come up with a more accurate statement.

- How were you taught, perhaps as a boy, to stand still, to not get too excited, to take it like a man? How do these common commands clash with your desire to pursue your dreams at full speed?

- Have you ever had the feeling that you were on hold, just treading water, or a bystander along the parade route of your own life? How do you deal with those feelings?

- The message of the prophet Haggai includes a description of the consequences of improper priorities. How do Kingdom priorities fit in with your current dreams and goals?

- Some people say that success itself is a sort of failure. Do you agree or disagree? How do you define success?

- What does it mean for you to have "a religious outlook on life"? How far along are you in this process?

- What kinds of answers about life's meaning have you received? Which ones have held some "hurt" for you?

■ Prayer Moments

Ask for prayer requests, and close with prayer. (**Leader:** See page 130 for a list of various approaches to group prayer.)

■ Suggestion for the Week Ahead

Think about your priorities this week. What would you really like to focus on? As the week goes by, compare your stated priorities with the priorities that you actually live out.

Make a list of some goals you've had in the past and ones you have for the future. Ask yourself: How do the goals I've had in the past influence my present goals and actions? In light of the way I'm living my life, what are my real priorities?

Wanting to Be Settled

■ Session Starter

Begin with this thought starter: "What was your 'security blanket' when you were a child?"

Ask the guys in your group to recall what they held onto as children. Some men will say it was an old blanket, toy, or stuffed animal. Others might mention family members or friends. Still others may not have had anything to hold onto.

After some group members have had a chance to talk about this, give each guy a sheet of paper and a pen. Invite each of them to write down one or two words that describe a present-day adult security blanket (for example: bank account, home equity, good job, loving family, health, skills and talents, education). Ask participants to write something other than "God"— something they're tempted to replace God with as their primary source of security. Invite volunteers to share what they've written before you move into the study.

■ One Man's Story

I lived in Chicago, right downtown. Life was often hectic, fast-paced, and draining. As I drove back from a trip in the country one day, it made sense to ask myself this question: Is it possible just to be content—just to *live*, without all the struggling and worrying?

I was headed back to the Windy City, driving through miles of cornfields in southern Illinois, passing through small towns separated by long stretches of flat state-road pavement. That day everything about those little towns looked so settled, peaceful, and serene. These quaint communities— each with a couple of white-steepled churches, inevitable grain elevator, rows of clapboard houses with perfectly manicured lawns and flower beds—spoke to me of a heavenly existence, far from the cacophony of train tracks and blaring sirens that would soon envelop me again. Surely these were places where a man and his family could live out their days in peace and warmth and love.

Imagine living in a place like this: Get up in the morning, go to work— in the fields or at the feed store—come home, play with the kids, sit in the lawn chair, watch the sun go down, and go to bed in peace. Hassle-free living, far from the rat race. Wow!

Of course, it's all a fantasy. For I knew that each picket-fenced yard harbored a house where real people lived, with all of their real problems and real struggles. If I could exchange my hectic pace for their seemingly tranquil existence, perhaps I would. But I know I'd just be inheriting a new set of problems. There's no escape from that.

The real question is: Is it wrong to seek contentment? Perhaps not, if I learn to give thanks that contentment in this life is just a fleeting preview to a better existence. For this is not yet home, no matter how hard I try to make it so. I'll always face a steep relational mountain to climb, a gut-wrenching trial, or a scary risk. It's called "living by faith." And I'm called to live that way whether I live in Chicago…or even if I move to a little house with a wooden porch that overlooks Route 55 and a few square miles of corn in Odell, Chenoa, Cayuga, or Gillum.

—Gary Wilde

■ God Enters the Story

Do not let your hearts be troubled. Trust in God; trust also in me. In my Father's house are many rooms; if it were not so, I would have told you. I am going there to prepare a place for you. And if I go and prepare a place for you, I will come back and take you to be with me that you also may be where I am. You know the way to the place where I am going.

—John 14:1-4

Now we know that if the earthly tent we live in is destroyed, we have a building from God, an eternal house in heaven, not built by human hands. Meanwhile we groan, longing to be clothed with our heavenly dwelling, because when we are clothed, we will not be found naked.

For while we are in this tent, we groan and are burdened, because we do not wish to be unclothed but to be clothed with our heavenly dwelling, so that what is mortal may be swallowed up by life. Now it is God who has made us for this very purpose and has given us the Spirit as a deposit, guaranteeing what is to come.

—2 Corinthians 5:1-5

Our citizenship is in heaven.

—Philippians 3:20a

■ The Story in Quotes

"This is the longing of all mankind—to have security, to know where one's place is. God created man and then he created a place for him, the Garden of Eden. When man lost God he lost at the same time his place. Since then, the longing for a place where he belongs…is in the heart of every human being."

—Walter Trobisch, quoted in the *Men's Devotional Bible*

"Desire can show itself as aching pain or delicious hope. Spirituality is, ultimately, about what we do with that desire. What we do with our longings, both in terms of handling the pain and the hope they bring us, that is our spirituality."

—Ronald Rolheiser, *The Holy Longing*

■ Can You Relate?

As a group, discuss these questions:

1. Which one of the three story sections in this study did you connect with most? Why?

2. As you read the story sections, did any of your own stories or experiences come to mind?

3. What other insights came to you? What questions did this study raise in your mind? Do you have any personal application you'd like to tell the group about?

4. What else would you like to say about this study's topic?

■ For Further Discussion

• Have you ever been to a place that you felt was "heavenly"? Talk about that.

• Does God really promise us continual bliss and happiness? Should we direct our energies toward trying to produce these conditions? Or can we learn to be content, even in the midst of daily chaos?

• How do you handle the longings and frustrations of "not being home yet"?

• Is the promise of heaven an encouragement to you to keep growing as a Christian? Or do you secretly dread the thought of your earthly life ending? Explain.

• Do you agree with Ronald Rolheiser that spirituality is about what we do with our desires? Why or why not?

■ Prayer Moments

Ask for prayer requests, and close with prayer. (**Leader:** See page 130 for a list of various approaches to group prayer.)

■ Suggestion for the Week Ahead

Take a period of fifteen to twenty minutes this week and direct your attention to this statement from Tim Hansel: "If you have to move even ten inches from where you are now in order to be happy, you never will be" (from "Points to Ponder," Reader's Digest, December 1992).

Now list the moves your family has made over the years. If possible, include dates, places, reasons for the moves, and your level of resulting happiness. Ask yourself the following questions:

• Which moves were likely according to God's will?

• Were any of the moves made because of boredom, restlessness, envy, status-seeking, or other questionable motives?

• How has God worked within all the moves to help me grow spiritually?

Living in the Power of Blessedness

■ Session Starter

Start your time together by briefly "blessing" one another. Here's how: As soon as everyone has gathered, let the men know that they will have the opportunity to go to at least one other man, shake his hand or place a hand on his shoulder, and say, "May the Lord…" They can complete the statement with an expression of desire or hope for that person. After the informal blessings, discuss:

- Who got blessed and who didn't? How did that feel?

- How important is it to know that you're blessed in others' eyes? How about in the eyes of God?

One Man's Story

Though it's been more than three decades since he died, I still want to know the man whose picture sits on my shelf—the young man with thick, wavy hair in the Air Force uniform, the one who looks a bit like me. Wouldn't knowing more about my human father, especially how he related with me many years ago, help me be more open to the blessings of my heavenly Father?

I think that the truth is, what I really want is my earthly father's blessing. I want to be held in the gaze of kind eyes with a look that says: "Son, you're so precious to me." When a father is absent—either physically or emotionally—we still crave that sense of blessedness no matter how old we are. Like the biblical Esau, who wailed, "Bless me—me too, my father!" the abandoned son continues to cry out in his lifelong search. I know I haven't outlived that need, nor have many of my men friends. And whether or not our fathers ever conveyed "I love you" to us, most of us still crave to see that deep sense of approval in their eyes.

In the movie *A River Runs Through It*, a minister's young son stands at the river's edge, launching his fly-cast bait expertly into the water. The father isn't content just to observe the skill of his son as he stands glorious in the sunlight; for the dad, it's a moment to utter a blessing. He says: "You are a fine fisherman." But later, after the son has been killed and the boy's brother states that all he really knew of the young man was that he was a fine fisherman, the father says: "You know more than that; he was *beautiful*."

Perhaps some of us know we're beautiful in our parents' eyes, but the rest of us haven't been so convinced. I can see that one of the great challenges of spiritual growth for me is to become aware of the ways—both healthy and self-destructive ways—that I seek to become beloved on the earth, to be seen as beautiful in the gaze of loving eyes.

—Gary Wilde

■ God Enters the Story

After Isaac finished blessing him and Jacob had scarcely left his father's presence, his brother Esau came in from hunting. He too prepared some tasty food and brought it to his father. Then he said to him, "My father, sit up and eat some of my game, so that you may give me your blessing."

His father Isaac asked him, "Who are you?"

"I am your son," he answered, "your firstborn, Esau."

Isaac trembled violently and said, "Who was it, then, that hunted game and brought it to me? I ate it just before you came and I blessed him— and indeed he will be blessed!"

When Esau heard his father's words, he burst out with a loud and bitter cry and said to his father, "Bless me—me too, my father!"

—Genesis 27:30-34

For the Lord's portion is his people, Jacob his allotted inheritance.

In a desert land he found him, in a barren and howling waste. He shielded him and cared for him; he guarded him as the apple of his eye, like an eagle that stirs up its nest and hovers over its young, that spreads its wings to catch them and carries them on its pinions. The Lord alone led him; no foreign god was with him.

He made him ride on the heights of the land and fed him with the fruit of the fields. He nourished him with honey from the rock, and with oil from the flinty crag, with curds and milk from herd and flock and with fattened lambs and goats, with choice rams of Bashan and the finest kernels of wheat.

—Deuteronomy 32:9-14

As soon as Jesus was baptized, he went up out of the water. At that moment heaven was opened, and he saw the Spirit of God descending like a dove and lighting on him. And a voice from heaven said, "This is my Son, whom I love; with him I am well pleased."

—Matthew 3:16-17

Praise be to the God and Father of our Lord Jesus Christ, who has blessed us in the heavenly realms with every spiritual blessing in Christ.

—Ephesians 1:3

■ The Story in Quotes

"The average man today remains trapped in his boyhood fear of abandonment, still believing in his broken heart that real manhood comes *from*, rather than *through* the earthly father. So he fears other men because they, too, seem to hold that awesome power over him, as his father did."

—Gordon Dalbey, *Healing the Masculine Soul*

"With my dad I feel a sense of continuity, like we're in the same race and he's passing on the baton. Talking about it sounds corny, but if I were sitting alone with my dad, it wouldn't be unusual for me to talk about how much I love him."

> —Jeff Bridges, actor, son of Lloyd Bridges, quoted in *Things I Should Have Said to My Father*, Joanna Powell, editor

"My dad had a left eye that twinkled out of control when he was happy. Making that happen was a key motivator in my life until the day he died."

> —Jim Lehrer, PBS news anchor, quoted in *Things I Should Have Said to My Father*, Joanna Powell, editor

■ Can You Relate?

As a group, discuss these questions:

1. Which one of the three story sections in this study did you connect with most? Why?

2. As you read the story sections, did any of your own stories or experiences come to mind?

3. What other insights came to you? What questions did this study raise in your mind? Do you have any personal application you'd like to tell the group about?

4. What else would you like to say about this study's topic?

■ For Further Discussion

- Note the forms of practical compassion that characterized God's relationship with his "son" Jacob (that is, the Hebrew people) in Deuteronomy 32:9-14. How have you experienced this kind of provision and care from God in your life?

- Give some reasons why it was important for Jesus to hear the blessing of his heavenly Father (Matthew 3:16-17) at the outset of his earthly ministry. What forms of blessing did you receive from your father (or other adults) as you grew up?

- How do you think men (like Esau) survive the absence of blessing from their fathers? How does Scripture offer healing in this regard? (Be as practical as possible in your response.)

- Reread the statement by Jeff Bridges. Would it be usual or unusual for you to talk with your dad about how much you love him? Why?

- As a child, could you make your dad's eyes twinkle? How? Is this a happy memory or not?

■ Prayer Moments

Ask for prayer requests, and close with prayer. (*Leader:* See page 130 for a list of various approaches to group prayer.)

■ Suggestion for the Week Ahead

Take some time this week to jot a list of the phrases that you heard in your household as you grew up. For example:

"Why can't you keep your room clean?"

"I like the way you smile."

"You dummy!"

"Good job!"

"Sure, I'll help you with that."

"Don't bother me right now!"

Go back and place a B or a C in front of each statement, to represent "blessing" or "curse." Are there more B's or more C's on your list? Then answer these questions for yourself: How much of a "blessing reservoir" or "curse reservoir" do I draw from as an adult? How does this affect my walk with God and my relationships with others?

Spend a few moments in prayer, thanking God for the blessings you know and asking him to help you forgive and counteract the "curses" you've endured over the years.

Just "Being"...With the Lord

■ Session Starter

Gather everyone into a circle, and tell group members that you're going to start your time in an unusual way—by being quiet together for five minutes. Let the men know that during the time of silence they don't need to talk to God or make any requests of him. Rather, they should simply acknowledge God's presence and become more aware of his fellowship and love.

As your silent time ends, read aloud Psalm 46:10a to refocus peoples' minds on the purpose for the silence: "Be still, and know that I am God."

After the period of silence, discuss this question:

• Why do we seem to do everything *except* "be still" in our lives?

■ One Man's Story

I once watched a Japanese tea ceremony, and I was struck with how aware the participants were of each other. This attitude seems so foreign to our culture. The participants in the tea ceremony sit still and silent on a straw mat, facing each other, waiting for the hissing sound of boiling water in the pot before them. They listen to the water seethe, tuning everything else out of their minds. One man drops in the tea and whisks it, then presents the pottery bowl to his friend. The receiver looks at the bowl, inspects it, feels it, comments about its beauty, and then slowly pours the tea into a mouth that tastes it—really tastes it. Everything is done slowly. Awareness reigns.

Of course they're not just drinking the tea. It sounds strange, but it's as if they're "being there with" the tea. Could I just "be there" when tea-drinking is what I'm doing? Sometimes I wonder: Can I even do one thing without a multitude of other things screaming for my attention?

Yet if I gather a few minutes out of this day to be quiet, I'm taking a dangerous risk: I may have to face myself. I'll have to live inside my own skin for a while. Will that be a welcome experience?

I've asked myself lately: What's so frightening about taking time to be still? One answer is that I may have to come to terms with my own defenses—the ways I avoid self-knowledge could become clearer; the feelings hidden just below the surface might pop up and demand a response. How inconvenient!

Instead, if I rush through my day as usual, my hurried gorging seems natural. If I'm feeling brutalized by deadlines, my coarse bickering with the kids or co-workers appears justified. And if I've had "important" work to do all day, then my escape in front of the TV all evening feels like a deserved retreat. Unless...

Unless I choose to be quiet—to be with myself in the presence of God. Then my behaviors become less reasonable. They may take on the look of rather shallow escape tactics.
—Gary Wilde

■ God Enters the Story

Be still, and know that I am God.
—Psalm 46:10a

The Lord said [to Elijah], "Go out and stand on the mountain in the presence of the Lord, for the Lord is about to pass by."

Then a great and powerful wind tore the mountains apart and shattered the rocks before the Lord, but the Lord was not in the wind. After the wind there was an earthquake, but the Lord was not in the earthquake. After the earthquake came a fire, but the Lord was not in the fire. And after the fire came a gentle whisper. When Elijah heard it, he pulled his cloak over his face and went out and stood at the mouth of the cave.
—1 Kings 19:11-13a

The apostles gathered around Jesus and reported to him all they had done and taught. Then, because so many people were coming and going that they did not even have a chance to eat, he said to them, "Come with me by yourselves to a quiet place and get some rest."

So they went away by themselves in a boat to a solitary place.
—Mark 6:30-32

As Jesus and his disciples were on their way, he came to a village where a woman named Martha opened her home to him. She had a sister called Mary, who sat at the Lord's feet listening to what he said. But Martha was distracted by all the preparations that had to be made. She came to him and asked, "Lord, don't you care that my sister has left me to do the work by myself? Tell her to help me!"

"Martha, Martha," the Lord answered, "you are worried and upset about many things, but only one thing is needed. Mary has chosen what is better, and it will not be taken away from her."
—Luke 10:38-42

■ The Story in Quotes

"We have developed a phobia of being alone."
—Erich Fromm

"If there is any focus that the Christian leader of the future will need, it is the discipline of dwelling in the presence of the One who keeps asking us, 'Do you love me?'...Contemplative prayer keeps us home, rooted, and safe, even when we are on the road."
—Henri J.M. Nouwen, *In the Name of Jesus*

"True Christian experience must always include a genuine encounter with God. Without this, religion is but a shadow, a reflection of reality, a cheap copy of the original...The spiritual giants of old were men who at some time became acutely conscious of the real Presence of God."
—A.W. Tozer

"What a thing it is to sit absolutely alone in the forest at night, cherished by this wonderful, unintelligent perfectly innocent speech, the most comforting speech in the world...It will talk as long as it wants, the rain. As long as it talks I am going to listen."
—Thomas Merton, quoted in *Warrior Wisdom*, Daniel Moore, editor

■ Can You Relate?

As a group, discuss these questions:

1. Which one of the three story sections in this study did you connect with most? Why?

2. As you read the story sections, did any of your own stories or experiences come to mind?

3. What other insights came to you? What questions did this study raise in your mind? Do you have any personal application you'd like to tell the group about?

4. What else would you like to say about this study's topic?

■ For Further Discussion

• Have you ever tried to make being "in the presence of the Lord" (see 1 Kings 19:11) a part of your devotional life? Talk about that.

• Why is stillness important if you want to hear God's "gentle whisper" in your life? What does this type of quietness mean for you in practical terms?

• Look at Mark 6:30-32. Why did Jesus take his disciples to a solitary place? Do you believe you can find "creative solitude"? What do you think that means?

• OK, you're a guy. But are you more of a Martha or a Mary in your approach to life? What do you think Jesus meant by, "Mary has chosen what is better"?

• Contemplative prayer involves taking time just to be in God's presence—without words. How much value do you place on talking to God? What about listening to God?

• What's going on in your life right now that needs your fuller awareness? Why?

■ Prayer Moments

Ask for prayer requests, and close with prayer. (**Leader:** See page 130 for a list of various approaches to group prayer.)

■ Suggestion for the Week Ahead

Consider having a devotional time this week in which you do nothing except simply wait in God's presence for a few minutes. Before you start, ask God to help you clear your mind and be completely tuned in to his presence.

Succeeding...or Failing?

■ Session Starter

Gather the men of your group in a circle, and ask them to close their eyes for a few minutes. Stand outside the circle, and say something like, "Imagine that I'm your father." Pause for a few seconds, then say, "I'm going to place my hands on each of your shoulders, but I want you to imagine that these are your own father's hands."

Now go around the circle, stand behind each man, and place your hands firmly on the shoulders of each. Say to each one: "[Name], I'm so very proud of you." Allow some time of silence each time so that the statement has impact.

When you've gone around the circle, invite reactions to the exercise. Then ask the following questions:

- When did you experience this type of affirmation from your father? Describe the event.

- Were there times you wished this had happened?

- What sense of either satisfaction or longing do you still have related to your father's (or mother's) approval?

Move into your discussion time by pointing out that feelings of success or failure can be tied to our sense of acceptance in the eyes of our parents. Invite your group to express their feelings about that statement, and then continue.

■ One Man's Story

A number of years ago, I walked into my old junior high school to say hello to my mom, who was serving as secretary to the principal. This was a surprise visit, and as soon as Mom saw me she called out to her boss: "Mr. Munns, do you remember my son, Gary?" The man did remember me from my student days, and he walked over for a handshake.

"Tell Mr. Munns what you're doing, Gary."

I happily launched into a description of my duties as a bus driver for the Orange County Welfare Department. I would take senior citizens and mental patients to various government offices. It was my first real job out of college. I knew it wasn't the greatest job, but it was decent work and I was content.

"No, Gary, tell him what you are *going* to be doing."

I'd been making plans to go to seminary and enter the ministry at some point. All I could think was, What I'm doing now isn't good enough, Mom? Isn't it good enough just to be your son, making an honest living?

Of course I realized that she must have been proud of me or she wouldn't have been so eager to re-introduce me to my old principal. But I also felt that she was a bit embarrassed of me, too—of my station in life at that point, anyway. To this day, these kinds of remembered scenes move me onto old, well-worn paths of mental self-torture as I wonder: Have I been a failure so far? Will I ever come to a place of peace about where I am in life? Why do I never feel as though I've done enough?

No matter how old we are, we always seem to long for our parents' complete approval—whether they're still alive or not. I know that I often try to salve that longing by mentally toting up my career accomplishments, imagining how they might stand up in the court of parental opinion. My own children are probably beginning to do the same thing.

Certainly, workaholics thrive on this raging inner quest for acceptance. One man I know put it this way: "I wish that just once I could have heard these words from my father: 'Son, I'm so very proud of you.' I think I could have learned to relax a little more in life—sit back and enjoy the ride a little more."

—Gary Wilde

■ God Enters the Story

Then Jesus came from Galilee to the Jordan to be baptized by John. But John tried to deter him, saying, "I need to be baptized by you, and do you come to me?"

Jesus replied, "Let it be so now; it is proper for us to do this to fulfill all righteousness." Then John consented.

As soon as Jesus was baptized, he went up out of the water. At that moment heaven was opened, and he saw the Spirit of God descending like a dove and lighting on him. And a voice from heaven said, "This is my Son, whom I love; with him I am well pleased."

—Matthew 3:13-17

His disciples urged him, "Rabbi, eat something."
But he said to them, "I have food to eat that you know nothing about."
Then his disciples said to each other, "Could someone have brought him food?"

"My food," said Jesus, "is to do the will of him who sent me and to finish his work.

—John 4:31-34

Serve wholeheartedly, as if you were serving the Lord, not men, because you know that the Lord will reward everyone for whatever good he does, whether he is slave or free.

—Ephesians 6:7-8

■ The Story in Quotes

"[Dad] never made it as a ballplayer, so he tried to get his son to make it for him. By the time I was ten, playing baseball got to be like eating vegetables or taking out the garbage. So when I was fourteen, I started to refuse. Can you believe that?"

—Kevin Costner, as Ray Kinsella, in the movie *Field of Dreams*

"The kind of work God usually calls you to is the kind of work (a) that you need most to do and (b) that the world most needs to have done. If you really get a kick out of your work, you've presumably met requirement (a), but if your work is writing cigarette ads, chances are you've missed requirement (b.)"

—Frederick Buechner, *Wishful Thinking*

■ Can You Relate?

As a group, discuss these questions:

1. Which one of the three story sections in this study did you connect with most? Why?

2. As you read the story sections, did any of your own stories or experiences come to mind?

3. What other insights came to you? What questions did this study raise in your mind? Do you have any personal application you'd like to tell the group about?

4. What else would you like to say about this study's topic?

■ For Further Discussion

- Do you agree that we long for our parents' approval long after we're adults? What's your own experience with that?

- During what stages of your life have you been most concerned with success and failure issues? How have you attempted to deal with any doubts about your "success"?

- In what ways did God's words help prepare Jesus for his mission on earth? Do you have a solid sense of your own father's pride in you? Tell why or why not.

- Discuss with one other guy in your group: When have you felt most like a failure? What objective facts and subjective feelings came into play? How do you think God viewed you at that time?

- Did you ever sense that your parents were trying to live out their dreams through your life? Explain. Do you have any indications that you're doing the same with your children?

■ Prayer Moments

Ask for prayer requests, and close with prayer. (**Leader:** See page 130 for a list of various approaches to group prayer.)

■ Suggestion for the Week Ahead

In a journal, your PDA, your paper calendar, or on a blank page at the back of your Bible, write your definition of success in life. Give this ample thought, and then think back over your life so far. Work on determining to what extent your dreams and goals have been motivated by the values that come through your definition. Think:

• What do I *say* I value most in life?

• In light of how I've lived so far, what do I *demonstrate* as my key values?

• What steps could I take to bring my *lived values* more into line with my *expressed values*?

Seeking Contentment...or Engineering Life?

■ Session Starter

Hand each person in the group an index card, and invite the men to write two very brief personal obituaries. On one side of the card, they should write: "How my life turned out, *assuming I had complete control of it* and could have made everything work out as I wanted it to." On the other side of the card, they should write: "How I think my life will actually turn out, as I seek to give control of my life to God."

When everyone is finished, invite volunteers to read their two imaginary obituaries. Ask them to explain similarities and contrasts. Then discuss this question:

• To what extent are you truly convinced that God has the best in mind for you?

■ One Man's Story

Not long ago, I went to my mailbox and pulled out one of those chain letters that promises a load of cash if I just send my name on to the next person in line along with a ten-dollar bill—or something like that! The purely rational side of me knows that these letters are scams, but they still appeal to another part of me that hopes to suddenly latch onto a sure thing.

I call this compulsive desire my "Ralph Cramden complex." I'm secretly on the lookout for the big win—some scheme that will earn me a quick buck or maybe even help me get rich quick. Poor Ralph kept trying, but his plans always backfired. It only took him a half-hour of *The Honeymooners* TV show each week to realize that he couldn't force things to turn out exactly the way he wanted them to be. Always, at the end of the show, he had to admit that his attempts to engineer his future only served to make him look foolish.

I'm the same way. On one hand, I'm constantly hit with schemes and temptations that tug at me to take control of my life, to work out things the way I want them to be. There's no end to the voices telling me that I can run my own life if I'll just sign on the dotted line and send in a small deposit upfront.

Yet, another voice is calling out to me too. It's the voice of the Spirit who lives within me, reminding me that I can rest in the hands of One who reminds me that the things of this life are temporary; he has a home waiting for me that's not of this world. He tells me I shouldn't become attached to the imperfect here and now, or else I can lose sight of the perfect future he has in store for me.

He calls me to learn contentment.

It's a tough call, isn't it? The first approach requires "life engineering"—trying to force events to be the way I want them to be (with absolutely no guarantees and frequent frustrations). The second approach calls me to a more trusting openness to life's way of gifting me beyond my shabby expectations. And really, can I ever create a world of satisfaction for myself rather than receive my happiness as a gift?

—Gary Wilde

■ God Enters the Story

I rejoice greatly in the Lord that at last you have renewed your concern for me. Indeed, you have been concerned, but you had no opportunity to show it. I am not saying this because I am in need, for I have learned to be content whatever the circumstances. I know what it is to be in need, and I know what it is to have plenty. I have learned the secret of being content in any and every situation, whether well fed or hungry, whether living in plenty or in want. I can do everything through him who gives me strength.

Yet it was good of you to share in my troubles.

—Philippians 4:10-14

■ The Story in Quotes

"Because we lack a divine Center our need for security has led us into an insane attachment to things. We must clearly understand that the lust for affluence in contemporary society is psychotic...because it has completely lost touch with reality. We crave things we neither need nor enjoy."

—Richard Foster, *Celebration of Discipline*

"The settled happiness and security which we all desire, God withholds from us by the very nature of the world: but joy, pleasure, and merriment he has scattered broadcast. We are never safe, but we have plenty of fun, and some ecstasy."

—C.S. Lewis, *The Problem of Pain*

"It's an old adage that the way to be safe is never to be secure. Each one of us requires the spur of insecurity to force us to do our best."

—Harold W. Dodds

■ Can You Relate?

As a group, discuss these questions:

1. Which one of the three story sections in this study did you connect with most? Why?

2. As you read the story sections, did any of your own stories or experiences come to mind?

3. What other insights came to you? What questions did this study raise in your mind? Do you have any personal application you'd like to tell the group about?

4. What else would you like to say about this study's topic?

■ For Further Discussion

- When are you most tempted to "scheme" your way through a situation? How do things usually work out?

- How difficult is it for you to trust God with your happiness? What does it actually mean for a man to "give up control" of his life?

- How can you maintain your enthusiasm and energy for earning a living yet still live by grace, receiving our life as a gift?

- How do Paul's statements about contentment help you or complicate the issue for you?

- How would your life need to change so that you could say: "I'm content"? or "I can do all things through Christ"? Describe that kind of life in practical terms, using your own work and family situation.

- What would it mean for you to become less attached to things?

■ Prayer Moments

Ask for prayer requests, and close with prayer. (*Leader:* See page 130 for a list of various approaches to group prayer.)

■ Suggestion for the Week Ahead

- If you're married, consider raising the topic of control versus trusting in God with your wife this week. Talk about ways you've tried to "engineer" your life in the past. Discuss how this has affected your marriage relationship. Think through changes you think might help.

- During a "quiet time" this week, open yourself to a new level of trust in Christ's love and provision for you. In silence, wait before him.

Feeling Tempted Again? Sexual Purity

■ Session Starter

Open your session by inviting guys to share answers to these questions:

• When you were a child, did your dad or another adult ever have the traditional "birds and bees" talk with you? What happened? How did it go?

After you hear some stories—some will likely be humorous—discuss these questions:

• Would you say that you grew up viewing sex as basically dirty or as a gift from God? How does this affect your attitude today?

If your group has become somewhat close, the men might want to share answers. Or you can encourage them to silently ponder why they answer the way they do.

■ One Man's Story

Every time I go into the local video store, I'm reminded how easy it is for any of us, with just a few steps in the wrong direction, to enter a whole world of unbridled lust. Even in respectable neighborhoods, video stores often provide "Adult" sections.

Of course in my calmer, more rational moments, I can feel outrage or at least look down on those who succumb to this form of dismal escapism. But there are times when I secretly want to do the same thing. If I could guarantee anonymity, I could easily follow my biology at the expense of my spirituality.

The Internet has made these temptations even more acute for many men. It is relatively anonymous and even more readily available.

The tough part about temptation is that every form of it promises relief from some kind of deprivation, spiritual alienation, aloneness, or the sense that I'm split off from a part of me that longs for sweet reunion. Sexual lust, especially, offers a few seemingly moments of bliss. In mindless ecstasy, I can become unified—pull all the fragments of my personality together, if only for a brief moment—assuming I'll never wake up.

Of course, the waking comes so immediately—then the shame, guilt, and stark re-entry of longing for something to fulfill me. And the cycle of temptation starts another round.

One thing that's helped me is to begin viewing sin in a different light—not as something I steel myself against when temptation hits, but as something I finally gain the *freedom* not to do, as I recognize its self-destructive effects.

For example, when I hunger for comfort in my loneliness, I need to be careful not to feed that hunger without going back to the pain that causes it to begin with. Otherwise I'll keep trying to fill that emptiness within me with things that won't satisfy it.

No doubt the best way out is this: Look at what's being offered and ask, calmly, "Is this what I *really* want?" Whenever I risk letting that question sink in, I sense a deeper need beneath my desire for some bright and shiny object so temptingly offered. The object of my temptation works insidiously to keep me from thinking, to keep me from feeling, to keep me at a distance from the true desires of my heart. Yes, then temptation begins to show its true colors: a mindless detour on the path to authentic fulfillment in the Lord.

—Gary Wilde

■ God Enters the Story

We know that the law is spiritual; but I am unspiritual, sold as a slave to sin. I do not understand what I do. For what I want to do I do not do, but what I hate I do. And if I do what I do not want to do, I agree that the law is good. As it is, it is no longer I myself who do it, but it is sin living in me. I know that nothing good lives in me, that is, in my sinful nature. For I have the desire to do what is good, but I cannot carry it out. For what I do is not the good I want to do; no, the evil I do not want to do—this I keep on doing. Now if I do what I do not want to do, it is no longer I who do it, but it is sin living in me that does it.

So I find this law at work: When I want to do good, evil is right there with me. For in my inner being I delight in God's law; but I see another law at work in the members of my body, waging war against the law of my mind and making me a prisoner of the law of sin at work within my members. What a wretched man I am! Who will rescue me from this body of death?

—Romans 7:14-24

One evening David got up from his bed and walked around on the roof of the palace. From the roof he saw a woman bathing. The woman was very beautiful, and David sent someone to find out about her. The man said, "Isn't this Bathsheba, the daughter of Eliam and the wife of Uriah the Hittite?" Then David sent messengers to get her. She came to him, and he slept with her. (She had purified herself from her uncleanness.) Then she went back home.

—2 Samuel 11:2-4

■ The Story in Quotes

"It is precisely the men and women who are dedicated to spiritual leadership who are easily subject to very raw carnality. The reason for this is that they do not know how to live the truth of the Incarnation. They separate themselves from their own concrete community."

—Henri Nouwen, *In the Name of Jesus*

"It is no accident, I think, that many lovers of God fall into illicit human love affairs…There is a kind of sexual addiction, I think, the roots of which are to be found in passionate love for God."

—Gerald G. May, *The Awakened Heart*

■ Can You Relate?

As a group, discuss these questions:

1. Which one of the three story sections in this study did you connect with most? Why?

2. As you read the story sections, did any of your own stories or experiences come to mind?

3. What other insights came to you? What questions did this study raise in your mind? Do you have any personal application you'd like to tell the group about?

4. What else would you like to say about this study's topic?

■ For Further Discussion

- Describe the ways you identify with the Apostle Paul's feelings in Romans 7:14-24 when it comes to areas of temptation in your life.

- Have you noticed any patterns or stress factors that tell you when you're most likely to be tempted with lust? What can you share about that?

- Do you agree that sexual desire can sometimes represent a misplaced spiritual longing? Explain.

- In your opinion, how well would it work to stop and ask yourself: "What do I really want?" at the beginning of lustful temptation?

- Have you ever had a "David and Bathsheba moment"? What's your advice to the other guys about how to handle those times of temptation? In other words, what works best for you or *doesn't* work well?

■ Prayer Moments

Ask for prayer requests, and close with prayer. (**Leader:** See page 130 for a list of various approaches to group prayer.)

■ Suggestion for the Week Ahead

If you're having a problem with lust and pornography, try a different approach in your prayers—perhaps a more honest approach. Instead of saying, "Lord, I don't want that; I never want to do it again," tell God what's really happening inside you: "This is who I am, Lord, a person who wants _____ so bad right now."

Be specific about what you want, what your body is longing for—even if it's crass or vulgar. Assume that God already knows about your desires and longings, and offer those desires to him.

CHAPTER 6 TOOLBOX

Prayer Record

As the men in your Bible study group spend time together in prayer, each participant can use a copy of this form to make notes about requests. As a group, periodically review this record to ask for updated information and to discover how God has answered your prayers. While it's a simple form, you'll experience amazing encouragement as you track how God is responding to your prayers.

Date	Request/Concern	Answer	Date Answered

Index of Scripture for Bible Studies

Use this list to find a ready-to-go Bible study focused on a specific verse.

RETREATS: BOYS JUST WANT TO HAVE FUN

As we sit down to review our golf scores at the clubhouse restaurant, Bob looks as if he's in pain. It has nothing to do with missed putts, shanked shots, or losing the match on the eighteenth hole. Bob has a different problem, and his pain is real.

Quite a few years ago, Mother Teresa made an appearance on the *Merv Griffin Show*. Most of the conversation was typical talk show chatter, but then Merv asked this interesting question: "What's the greatest problem in the world?" You'd think her answer would involve world hunger, the cold war, poverty, or the potential for nuclear holocaust. But she answered with none of these. Mother Teresa's response was a single word: "loneliness."

That word describes Bob's problem. He had cared for a sick wife for ten years until she quietly passed away. Now he's alone. In fact, Bob is lonely. He'd like to remarry someday, but in the meantime he looks for friendship. I'm his friend. We retreat weekly to the golf course. There he finds a relationship that helps fill his loneliness, at least for a time.

You've read a number of times in these pages that men need to develop strong relationships with other men—friendships where we can be admired, respected, helped, challenged, and encouraged. Someone once said to me that if you're not being admired by another man, then you're hurting.

Ecclesiastes 4:8-12 emphasizes the importance of building reliable relationships with other men:

> There was a man all alone; he had neither son nor brother. There was no end to his toil, yet his eyes were not content with his wealth. "For whom am I toiling," he asked, "and why am I depriving myself of enjoyment?" This too is meaningless—a miserable business!
>
> Two are better than one, because they have a good return for their work: If one falls down, his friend can help him up. But pity the man who falls and has no one to help him up! Also, if two lie down together, they will keep warm. But how can one keep warm alone? Though one may be overpowered, two can defend themselves. A cord of three strands is not quickly broken.

Men have always sought out teams for life's adventures:

- Lewis and Clark explored unsettled parts of this country together.

- Sir Edmund Hillary and Tenseng Norgay climbed Mount Everest together.

- In the Old West, wagon trains circled together to provide safety from attack.

- In ancient Israel, David's and Jonathan's hearts were knit together.

- In the Gospels, we read that Jesus and his disciples walked, talked, and prayed together.

One of my favorite movies is *City Slickers*. Mitch and his friends from the big city head to the wild West for adventure, challenge, and fun. Their experiences wouldn't have been the same if they hadn't shared the time with friends.

Boys like to have fun together. So do men. When I was a boy growing up in Indiana, we played sandlot baseball. I spent my summer hours from dawn till dusk playing baseball with my friends. Baseball was fun, but the cool part of that experience was the friends.

In Designs for Fund-Raising, Harold "Sy" Seymour writes that human beings have two fundamental needs. One is "to be sought"; the other is to be a "worthwhile member of a worthwhile group."[1] While most of us probably have more than two basic needs, he's right about the importance of these two. On the sandlot, the worst thing that could happen was to be chosen last for a team. The second worst was winding up on a team with no chance of winning.

Church ought to be a place where we're sought out as men. Church is the place where we can always win. The body of Christ can provide exactly the right structure for affirmation and team spirit.

When you share an experience with others, the activity or event is more meaningful and lasting. Maybe you remember the quick friendships you made at church camp or in Boy Scouts when you were a kid. Or maybe you've been able to participate in short-term mission trips as an adult. In these situations, your life is inexplicably woven together with others who experience the same tragedies, hardships, challenges, and joys you're going through. Your hearts are molded to one another as you laugh, cry, share, work, sacrifice, and celebrate together.

Done properly, a men's retreat is an ideal way to bring men together for this kind of meaningful and lasting experience. Away from the routines of life, men can be men, without pretense. They can laugh, cry, celebrate, and worship loudly and off key without inhibition.

The key to doing retreats is doing them right. Plenty has been written about the proper atmosphere for men's ministry—allowing men to be men. An attitude of acceptance that we are men on a journey, each at a different stage in our spiritual maturity, is an essential foundation for a successful retreat. With that as a given, let's focus on the practical aspects of putting on a great event.

First, a brief disclaimer: Much of what follows grows out of planning retreats for larger men's groups that require extensive planning and logistics. If you have a smaller group of men (say, fewer than twelve), and you're not inviting men from outside your church to join you, then you don't need to do everything suggested here to have a great men's retreat. However, many of the principles apply to any size event. Simply pick and choose what works for your group.

There are five parts or stages to the practical process of building a successful retreat—preparation, planning, promotion, production, and post-mortem. The order's important. So, let's begin with the first step.

1. Preparation

I used to run capital fund-raising campaigns for charities. One of the first steps in a campaign is to determine if an organization is ready for that approach. If there wasn't already a core of steady donors, the organization had little chance to succeed at the large undertaking of a capital campaign.

The same is true for a men's retreat. You need to determine your group's readiness for this event. If you have just a few leaders you can count on, you're probably not ready to pull off a huge event. Of course, there's no reason you can't hold a smaller retreat; perhaps instead of inviting a big-name speaker, you could create a small-group atmosphere.

Also keep in mind that if a retreat is your only men's activity of the year, you don't really have a men's ministry. It would just be a men's event. A retreat should be an outgrowth of the ongoing and regular ministry activities you carry out to reach and build men. It's part of a mix of methods you're using. If you have a great foundation in place with small groups and regular men's gatherings, a retreat can be a great asset for taking men deeper. A retreat allows men to disconnect from the routines of life. It provides shared experiences and time to concentrate on special areas of need. The vision for the event must grow from the desire to take men deeper as followers of Christ and to be committed to the welfare of each other.

■ Prayer Support

"Much prayer, much power. Little Prayer, little power." If you want to be prepared for a ministry of any kind, you must invest in "much prayer." Before you lift a finger to do anything, find a core group of men who will commit to praying that God will lead and empower your team. As men, that's hard for us on two levels. First, we're problem solvers—we want to take matters into our own hands and get on with it. Second, since we talk to transmit information, we usually communicate using the least number of words possible.

Most of us are men of few words—if we pray at all, we don't pray much. But like all the aspects of your men's ministry, planning a retreat needs to begin by talking with God, listening to his Spirit, and discerning his plan.

Involve other groups in your church. Ask the women's ministry, senior adults, the youth group, and others to pray for God's direction for this experience. Provide a prayer request list to help others pray more specifically for your team. A typical prayer list might include asking God to

- provide the appropriate leader;

- create a greater desire within us to minister to men;

- save us from the distractions of passions other than God, family, and calling;

- lead us to the resources that can make the retreat a life-changing experience;

- help us to define our purpose for this event;

- direct us to a speaker who will connect with our men;

- help us find a theme that will draw men to the retreat; and

- lead the right men to attend the retreat.

■ Retreat Chairman

Do you have a champion for this event? You need someone with a contagious passion, good leadership skills, and a vision for what the retreat can do for men. Second, are there others who will willingly take on assignments to make the retreat happen? The vision for the event must be shared by more than one person—even though there will be one primary leader.

Once you've found a man to lead, he can assist in recruiting committee or task force chairmen. The head of each task force will also serve on the executive committee for the event. The reality is that the more men you can involve in the planning aspects of the event, the more men you'll have at the event. The whole process of working together to put together the retreat also offers men the opportunity to serve together and to grow into expanded leadership positions.

Develop a job description for this position. This might be a task the overall leaders of your men's ministry take on before you search for a retreat chairman. As in a typical job description, outline the qualifications for the position along with the expectations and the line of accountability.

Here are some of the characteristics you'll want the retreat chairman to possess:

- leadership skills

- the ability to motivate others to action

- a strong commitment to Christ

- the ability to overcome adversity—a "can do" kind of guy

- a thick skin (not everyone will like everything at the retreat)

- an ability to delegate responsibility and authority

The duties of the chairman include:

- providing overall direction of the retreat

- recruiting the task force chairmen

- supervising the task force chairmen

- reporting to designated leaders (for example, men's ministry leadership team, pastor, and church board)

- serving as spokesman for the retreat—ready to answer questions about the event

- attending the retreat to see that it accomplishes its purpose and to help deal with the unexpected

■ Committees

Depending on how large your church and men's group are, you may need to combine some of the following roles and task forces. If you have enough men to fill all the separate assignments, that's a great way to get more men to take ownership for the event's success. In a smaller church, you might have one man responsible for each of these areas rather than a committee. Adapt and combine these to fit your situation.

- administration/finance

- prayer

- facilities/logistics

- recreation/activity

- program

- promotion

Let's look at the overall responsibilities for each of these groups.

Administration/Finance task force. This group oversees details related to any contractual arrangements for facilities, speakers, music groups, and so forth. With the input from leaders and other task forces, this group creates and monitors the retreat budget. Keeping accurate records for accounting purposes is vital. The registration process may also be the responsibility of this task force.

In a larger church, this committee should be large enough to provide internal accountability, which probably means three or four men. In a smaller church, be sure to think of how you can build in checks and balances if only one or two men are overseeing these responsibilities.

Prayer task force. It's not enough to be praying before you start planning your retreat. Continue to pray throughout all phases of the retreat process. Ideally, one of the members of this group should attend meetings of each of the other task forces to be aware of specific prayer needs that emerge. In addition, it would be great to have a representative from other areas of ministry in your church take part in this important task force—the women's ministry, youth ministry, and senior adult ministry, for example. Not only is prayer critical as the retreat is being planned and promoted, it's essential while the retreat is going on. Challenge this task force to recruit people who can pray during the days of the retreat.

Facilities/logistics task force. A good bed and great food are key components to getting men to return to a retreat year after year. The facilities/logistics task force deals with all the details of "hosting" the event. Where will it be held? What driving directions do men need to find it? What are the audiovisual requirements? What transportation and hosting needs does the speaker require? What will the group eat during meals and breaks?

Recreation/activity task force. Remember that men like to have fun together. But not everyone likes the same kinds of activities. This task force makes sure that the retreat provides a variety of activities for a variety of guys. This task force will need to communicate with the facilities task force to ensure that those options are available for the men at the locations being considered. Does the facility have all the equipment needed for activities, or does the church need to bring along "toys for the boys"?

Program task force. If you've been to a workshop, seminar, or retreat, you already know that the program can make or break the event. This committee will be responsible for the content of the weekend's program—including hiring a speaker, arranging for music, coordinating group activities, and ensuring program flow. If possible, include the leader responsible for service planning at your church each week. This person has experience in how to move a service along and how to seamlessly move from one part of a program to another. The program should have a sense of momentum; you don't want things to peak too early in terms of intensity. You also want variety in the program—again to provide something meaningful for the different types of guys who attend. It isn't wise to try to keep every component of the program at a high-energy level. This group needs to plan about how to integrate meditative times with periods of inspiration and more energetic worship.

This group should also appoint a good "upfront" man to be master of ceremonies. This emcee will be responsible, at least in a public way, for maintaining the flow and timing of the event program.

Promotion task force. You can have the best program, held at the best facility, terrific recreational opportunities, but it's almost pointless if no one shows up. While it's up to all task force members as well as the leaders of your overall men's ministry to recruit attendees, it falls to the promotion task force to come up with a strategy to communicate the event in ways that will attract the most men possible. This includes designing bulletin inserts and brochures, handling pulpit announcements, creating PowerPoint presentations, and carrying out other promotional activities. See Toolbox page 193 for "Men's Retreat Promotion Timeline." This checklist will help the promotion task force stay on track.

Final preparation hint: At the outset of preparing for the retreat, begin building a "Retreat Operations Manual" The chairman can collect minutes and copies of documents from various task forces and put together a file or three-ring binder along with his own notes. This will make it easier to recruit the chairman for next year's retreat. It also provides a record of procedures and agreements to help ensure excellent events in the future.

2. Planning

Planning is a matter of counting the cost, assessing the manpower, and gathering the information necessary to make good decisions. It's biblical to plan. Luke reminds us that thinking ahead about important decisions is critical: "Suppose one of you wants to build a tower. Will he not first sit down and estimate the cost to see if he has enough money to complete it? For if he lays the foundation and is not able to finish it, everyone who sees it will ridicule him, saying, 'This fellow began to build and was not able to finish' " (Luke 14:28-30).

Probably the best way to facilitate overall planning for the retreat is to create an executive committee made up of the chairmen of the task forces. The retreat chairman leads the executive committee, and he may ask other individuals to be part of the executive committee. This committee is also a good place for your men's ministry leadership team to plug in; ask someone from among those leaders to sit in on the retreat executive committee's meetings.

Every effective expedition requires thorough advance planning. You wouldn't consider setting out on a camping trip with no thought about a tent, the things you need for a campfire, and other supplies. Don't make the mistake of thinking that all you have to do is decide when and where you'll meet and men will automatically show up and have a productive time. You need to carefully plan to cover all the details that make for a great event. Several components of the retreat demand advance thought and planning, such as

- Who'll take on what responsibilities?

- Who's in charge?

- What will the theme be?

- Who will be the best speaker for your men right now?

- Where will you meet?

- What will the schedule be?

- How will you generate the maximum attendance?

- What budget will be required?

- What will you charge for registration?

- What recreational activities are planned and included?

- What contingency plans do you have in case of unusual occurrences, such as a speaker who doesn't show up or a weekend of rain?

The balance of this section deals with the above questions.

■ Theme

The preparation phase for your event has already dealt with selecting the men who will lead and carry out the details of your retreat. But in the planning stage, you'll want to decide on a theme for the event. Here are some themes that have been used at other men's retreats:

- Being Men on Purpose

- Mighty Men of God

- Taking Up the Cross

- Boot Camp for God

- Raising the Banner

- Tough Love

- Building Confident Men

- Seasons of Life

- The Time of Your Life

- Men on Task

- Hitting the Mark

- Iron Sharpening Iron

- Jack of all Trades and Master of Some

- Letting Go and Letting God

- Locking Arms

Choosing a theme makes for a fun brainstorming session. In less than a half hour, your planning committee will come up with many variations for a theme. One key point to remember when choosing a theme is how it will affect the promotional phase. Put yourself in the shoes of someone who hasn't been a part of the planning team—someone who doesn't have your background about the objective for the retreat. Words mean things, so it's wise to carefully consider what message you're communicating with your theme. If it sounds too intimate, you probably won't attract men who fear they'll be asked to open up to men they don't really know. (The thought that scares a man even more than being put on the spot to share his innermost feelings with a stranger is being forced to listen to a stranger share his!) At the same time, a retreat can be a great place for men to go deeper in already budding relationships, so you do want your theme to carry meaning as well. Some of the most attractive themes have to do with active and practical ways men can better themselves.

You might even want to pull together a small, informal focus group to see how men react to your theme. This will help you make sure you're communicating what you really want to say about the retreat. Consider asking men from another church to participate in this way. The theme you select will be with you until the last minute of the retreat, so choose carefully.

■ Schedule

Your schedule should help you achieve the purpose of the retreat. Be sure to include flextime and free time so men can choose their own activities. This is particularly critical for younger guys, who like to have choices and options. Don't design the schedule so tightly that it can't change based upon unexpected blessings or challenges at the retreat. However, it's critical to start and end sessions on time, and for men to know what's ahead. Reveal the "playbook" at the beginning of the retreat so guys will know what to expect. Check out the "Sample Retreat Schedule" on Toolbox page 187.

■ Speakers

One key factor that can make or break your retreat is the speaker. This is who God will use to touch hearts and connect with the men. One of the most important qualities of a speaker is that he's truly in tune with the needs of men. Is he transparent in his presentation? Does he help listeners apply what he's talking about? Does he approach topics in a fun and entertaining way? Does he get to the heart of what your guys need to hear? Does he only do "canned" presentations, or is he willing to adapt his presentations to the theme of your retreat?

In terms of finding a speaker, you might first consider your own pastor or associate pastor. This could be a time to get to know this person better in a casual setting. You might even provide a question-and-answer time following each talk. Or consider a pastor from a neighboring church; you could work out an arrangement to have your pastor speak at that church's men's retreat.

Another option is seeking an outside speaker. Contact other churches in your area or your association or denomination headquarters for recommendations. Or contact one of the scheduling agencies that represents nationally known speakers. See "Christian Speaker Resources" on Toolbox page 188. You could also tap into a parachurch men's ministry organization; many of these use seminar formats that can easily be adapted to a weekend retreat. See "Men's Ministry Organizations" on Toolbox page 190 for a list of organizations that present their material in the context of church men's retreats.

When you've narrowed down your choices to two or three speakers who are available on the dates you're holding your retreat, ask for audiotapes or videotapes of previous presentations for your program task force to review. Note if the speaker uses a variety of teaching methods, such as group activities, interactive exercises, audiovisual tools, outlines, and notebooks. The men in your group have different learning styles; effective speakers will try to accommodate these styles by varying their methods to enhance communication.

▮ Location

Part of the concept of a retreat is "retreating"—getting away from the "normal" aspects of life. If you hold the retreat at your church facilities, there are too many distractions. If participants go home for the night, it can break their concentration on the purpose for the weekend. Others will get caught up in duties that face them and wind up missing part of the retreat. Find a location away from your church—and even away from your community. A camp, conference or retreat center, or hotel within a two-hour drive from your community helps ensure that guys get away from it all, stay for the whole event, and concentrate on the task at hand.

Here are some factors to consider as you're choosing a facility for your retreat.

- accessibility
- lodging type (for example, a rustic campground versus a hotel)
- meeting space (capacity and "fit" for your program)
- recreational facilities
- pricing
- reputation of food service
- general atmosphere
- availability of audiovisual equipment
- flexibility of staff and service orientation

Realize up front that you can't please everyone when it comes to location. Some guys like the idea of roughing it in a camp setting. Others feel like something less than a full-service hotel is roughing it. Think about what location will attract as many guys as possible, and seek to find some middle ground.

In his book *How to Build a Life-Changing Men's Ministry*, Steve Sonderman offers this counsel about retreat facilities: "Use a facility where the accommodations are appropriate for men of all ages. I have been to rustic retreats where it was difficult to sleep. Needless to say, that doesn't go over well with most men. A nicer camp or even a hotel is a better place for a retreat."

Some locations offer a variety of lodging options—from camping to cabins to hotel-style rooms. You can reflect these choices on the registration form and in the pricing. If some guys don't want to rough it in sleeping bags, they have a more comfortable choice. If this isn't possible, be sure to communicate in your promotional material what type of lodging you'll have. Some men won't want to go rustic and will be disappointed to sign up, pay their fee, and then find out they have to bring their own bedding. Allow guys to make that choice so they don't feel tricked into going and not enjoy the time away. Your registration form can also allow guys to request preferred roommates. If you have small groups established already in your church, you might look for a location with cabins that would allow groups to bunk together.

■ Picking a Date

Summer is rarely a good time for a men's retreat. Family vacations, reunions, and other family events conflict with summer retreats. The best three months of the year for a men's retreat seem to be May, September, and October. Announce the date at least six months in advance so men can get it on their calendars early. Many churches announce the date for an annual retreat within weeks after their current retreat, even if they don't have other details confirmed at that point.

■ Costs

Many decisions about your retreat will be governed by the budget. The largest expenses will be speaker, facility, and food costs. Figure out those three, and you'll have 80 percent of your budget covered. When you have a budget plan put together, you can set the pricing for the event and move ahead with other decisions. See "Building a Retreat Budget" Toolbox page 192 for a list of items that require some advance thought and planning.

Some churches subsidize retreats to keep costs down, which encourages more men to attend. Others reflect the actual cost but solicit donations for financial aid so that more men can attend. It's important for men to pay something to attend even if they're not able to pay everything. When guys put money into something, they're much more likely to look for a return on their investment. The message in our culture is "If it's free, it's not worth much."

■ The Unexpected

Having a plan for the unexpected will save a lot of heartburn and panic. If you have a lot of outdoor recreational activities planned and the weather turns sour, you'll want to have some alternatives. Or what if, for some reason (legitimate or not), the speaker doesn't show up? What would you do? If you have a backup plan for emergencies, you won't sweat quite so much.

Throughout the planning phase, document everything you can in writing. Most speakers will want a signed agreement. The facility you choose will likely have a contract for you to sign. Read it carefully, and negotiate any potential areas of dispute in advance. You should push to get contractual agreements even if the other parties claim that they're not necessary. Make sure agreements include how you and the other parties will resolve any disputes that unexpectedly arise. The best way to avoid misunderstandings is to assume nothing and confirm everything in writing.

■ Registration

You don't have a registration until you have a *paid* registration. Collect fees when guys register—offer a discount for early registration. Guys will be more likely to attend if they register and pay early. They'll also be more likely to mention their plans to other men, who may decide to come along. (We do share a herd mentality.)

The registration form should include all the pertinent information that you will need from the men. You may want to add some additional information such as notation of any medical conditions and emergency contact numbers. Or if your retreat allows for a variety of lodging choices, the form can provide for communication of that preference as well.

3. Promotion

Obviously, you want to promote the retreat in positive and exciting ways, building momentum as you go. You can make the very first announcement without a lot of details. It can be as simple as a "save the date" pulpit announcement and Sunday bulletin statement. It should create, however, a sense of anticipation.

One church creates a Top Ten List à la *The Late Show* with David Letterman. This list can be humorous, serious, or a combination. For example, here are the top ten reasons a man should attend your men's retreat.

10. Where else can you go to play golf while telling your wife it is mainly a spiritual experience—and be right!

9. Great speaker.

8. Relevant topics.

7. Terrific location.

6. Recreational activities.

5. Break in routine.

4. Opportunity to grow closer to Christ.

3. Get to know other men in a nonthreatening environment.

2. Have honest and open discussions on important issues.

1. Eat all the junk food you want without guilt.

I remember a successful advertising promotion from when I was a child growing up in the Chicago area. A strong male voice would come on the radio and state, "I will bring a mountain to Chicago!" Everyone I knew heard the commercial, but no one had any idea what it was about. Some didn't even realize it was advertising. After months of speculation it was finally revealed—the product was Folgers Mountain Grown coffee. While pretty simple and a little corny, it was a successful campaign because it created conversation and a desire to know more about what was coming. Your most effective promotion plan will do the same.

While there are many ways you can and should promote the retreat, there's one method more powerful than any other. It's a one-to-one invitation one guy extends to another guy. Nothing else will come close to the impact of one man saying to another, "I'm going to our men's retreat, and it'd be great if you could join me." Of course, one key to creating that kind of atmosphere is putting together such a desirable event that no one will want to be left out—and no one will want his friend to miss it either.

Advertising experts understand that it takes five touches or exposures to get one response. So don't rely on just one method to communicate your retreat. In addition to the verbal announcement from the pulpit, the bulletin blurb, and a sign-up table in the foyer, leave no stone unturned in trying to communicate the excitement of your retreat and the importance of early registration. Here are a couple of suggestions.

- Create quality printed material. Make sure your posters, bulletin inserts, tickets, brochures, and banners all consistently reflect the theme of the retreat and the quality of the event. Promotional pieces often provide the first impression of what the event will be like. Make them good; bad first impressions are hard to overcome.

- Use technology. We live in a high-tech world, so use it. Create a PowerPoint presentation to promote the retreat. Videotape guys who attended last year's retreat as they explain what they got out of it. While you're thinking about it, plan to do some videotaping of this year's retreat so you have the resources for promoting it next year.

Turn to Toolbox page 193 for a basic "Men's Retreat Promotion Timeline." This checklist will ensure that you take every opportunity to let men know about the retreat.

4. Production

The next important phase of pulling your retreat together involves the on-site program and logistics. Here are the major tasks that need to take place at the event:

- Setup—for example the platform, lighting, sound, tables and seating, sales table if resources are offered, registration area, and decorations
- Check-in process—for example, lodging assignments; name tags; registration and money collection; and agenda, notebook, and pen distribution
- Master of ceremonies schedule—for example, program flow and announcements
- Audiovisual needs and schedule
- Meals and break arrangements
- Seating for various meetings—at tables or theater style
- Recreation arrangements
- Small-group formation

It will take a good crew of volunteers who are well acquainted, in advance, with their assignments to handle all the production and logistical aspects smoothly. Be careful not to overload one or two people with responsibilities.

In terms of what's going on during the retreat, think about how you'll handle a couple of other important areas:

■ Provide an Opportunity for Response

Make sure you give men a chance to respond to what they hear through a public response, meeting with someone for counseling, or a follow-up card they can complete and turn in. Men often make critical spiritual decisions at retreats. Have a plan in place for how you'll help them cement these important personal commitments.

■ Musical Note

Many churches use their own worship team or music and worship director; some contract with an outside leader. Make sure that the music is familiar to the men. Men's groups sometimes find it uncomfortable to sing, and if they're unsure about the songs it will be *very* awkward. Don't use the retreat to teach new songs. And make sure words are projected or printed so that everyone can see them.

Match the mood of the music to the event. For example, if a high-energy speaker is coming up, make sure the song preceding the speaker is upbeat. If a speaker has closed with a solemn challenge, follow up with a slower and more reflective song.

5. Postmortem

Not only do the retreat leaders and/or task forces need to debrief, be sure to communicate that you want the input and feedback of all who attended.

Survey the men at the end of the event while the experience is fresh. To increase participation, give away a prize to someone whose name you draw from the surveys that are turned in. Make the prize enticing enough that men will want to enter—perhaps something like a weekend retreat at a nearby hotel for the winner and his wife or tickets to an upcoming sporting event or concert. Check out Toolbox page 195 for a "Retreat Follow-Up Survey."

Hold a planning committee meeting within two weeks following the event to debrief members on everything that occurred leading up to and at the retreat.

- How did the task forces work?

- What can be done better next year?

- What common comments did retreat participants express in the surveys?

- What went really well?

- What kind of commitments did the men make?

Try to stay positive, but don't deny weaknesses either. However, criticism isn't the goal. Instead, identify areas for improvement and make plans to implement improvements for the next retreat.

Final Thoughts

Little things make a big difference. If you have doubts about this, just ask the boy who shared his lunch with Jesus! Often we focus on how God multiplied a few loaves and fishes. But we forget about the boy. He gave all that he had for lunch. He gave all he possessed at that moment, and God did something wonderful with it. God can take your humblest of efforts—if they're truly sacrificial and from the right motives—and do something wonderful at your men's retreat.

Little things make big differences in other ways, too. What distinguishes a great retreat from a good one is often found in the little extras—the attention to details. When delivered with excellence, seemingly small things can add up to a large result in terms of the retreat's atmosphere. Going the extra mile makes a big difference.

Retreats are about making a difference in men's lives. While it's fine to create fun experiences and good memories, the real purpose is to see men who are transformed. Perhaps some of the following comments from men who've attended retreats will inspire and excite you to prepare, plan, and pray for God to work and bring about the changes he desires in the lives of your men.

- "Camaraderie, fellowship, bonding—whatever you want to call it—is jump-started during men's retreats. [A retreat] is a great catalyst for the kind of friendship that the Bible describes as 'iron sharpens iron.' "

- "Although I did not give my testimony at the men's retreat, hearing the testimonies of men who I only knew casually has allowed me to bond with these men in a much deeper Christian fellowship. The trust and respect I have for these new friends has allowed opportunities for shared ministries through our church family."

- "I have realized that I am not alone—that other men share the same (sometimes secret) struggles that I have."

- "I have experienced a level of transparency that doesn't often occur outside of these venues."

- "There is something about joining together with other *men* which is more invigorating than a mixed group. There is a feeling of kindred spirit and camaraderie. I am inspired to be a man—one who loves God, his family, and his world. I always come away from men's retreats with a renewed vision and inspiration to lead my family in the fear and love of God."

- "I have been to two men's retreats with our church. Both were great spiritual "recharges," and I thoroughly enjoyed the fellowship and meeting guys I didn't know or know well. Very rewarding and life changing."

- "As a recent organizer of a men's retreat (as well as a participant, obviously), I continue to be amazed by how God works through these events to unify and heal Christian men. The world demands that men demonstrate their independence and self-sufficiency; during men's retreats and gatherings we learn that even the most successful among us have a desperate need for a relationship with God. It is not a weakness to rely on a strong foundation in the Lord, and we're not weird to be pursuing holiness. At men's retreats, I learn that there are lots of men who love Jesus, and I'm humbled to be one of them!"

The theme in these is obvious. God meets men on retreat and demonstrates his power in their lives to bring about change, challenge, and hope. God will bless those who attend your men's retreat and he'll certainly bless you and others who help put together this important event.

Jim Neal

Jim Neal is president of Dad the Family Shepherd (www.dtfs.org), an organization that challenges fathers to live out biblical values. He and his wife, Ruth, live in Maumelle, Arkansas. They have four grown children and fifteen grandchildren.

Endnotes

1. In his book *Designs for Fund-Raising,* Seymour credits Dr. Lawrence C. Kolb with the idea "that what people want most is simply 'to be sought.' " And he credits Dr. Dorothea C. Leighton with the idea that "every individual needs to feel that he is a 'worthwhile member of a group.' "

CHAPTER 7 TOOLBOX

Sample Retreat Schedule

Friday

6:00 p.m.–7:00 p.m.—Registration

7:30 p.m.–8:00 p.m.—Refreshments and fellowship (icebreaker)

8:00 p.m.–8:30 p.m.—Praise and worship

8:30 p.m.–10:00 p.m.—Session #1/small-group discussion

10:00 p.m.–? Informal fellowship and game time

Saturday

7:00 a.m.–7:30 a.m.—Morning prayer meeting

8:00 a.m.–8:40 a.m.—Breakfast

8:40 a.m.–9:00 a.m.—Praise and worship

9:00 a.m.–10:30 a.m.—Session #2/small-group discussion

10:30 a.m.–11:00 a.m.—Refreshment break

11:00 a.m.–12:00 p.m.—Session #3/small-group discussion

12:00 p.m.–5:30 p.m.—Lunch and free time

5:30 p.m.—Dinner

7:00 p.m.–7:30 p.m.—Praise and worship

7:30 p.m.–9:00 p.m.—Session #4/small-group discussion

9:00 p.m.—Saturday night campfire and fellowship

Sunday

8:00 a.m.–9:00 a.m.—Breakfast

9:15 a.m.–9:30 a.m.—Praise and worship

9:30 a.m.–10:00 a.m.—Message

10:00 a.m.–10:30 a.m.—Communion service

10:30 a.m.—Check out and departure

Christian Speaker Resources

■ The National Coalition of Men's Ministries

180 Wilshire Blvd.
Casselberry, FL 32707
Phone: (407) 332-7703
Toll free: 1-877-MAN-NCMM (626-6266)
E-mail: Office@ncmm.org
Web site: www.ncmm.org

■ Christian Speakers & Artists Agency

118 Seaboard Lane
Ste. 100
Franklin, TN 37067
Phone: (615) 771-9400
Toll free: 1-800-220-8125
Fax: (615) 261-1062
E-mail: info@csaagency.com
Web site: www.christianspeakers.com

■ MVP Speakers

445 Courtney Lane
Matthews, NC 28105
Phone: (704) 849-2838
Toll free: 1-800-943-3888
Fax: (704) 844-0941
E-mail: rwussports@aol.com
Web site: www.mvpspeakers.com

■ Nashville Speakers Bureau

P.O. Box 110909
Nashville, TN 37222-0909
Phone: (615) 263-4143
Fax: (615) 263-4146
E-mail: info@nashspeakers.com
Web site: www.faithbasedspeakers.com

■ The Robinson Agency

1946 Kensington High St.
Lilburn, GA 30047-2524
Phone: (770) 736-0775
Toll free: 1-800-782-2995
E-mail: contact@therobinsonagency.com
Web site: www.TheRobinsonAgency.com

TOOLBOX
Speakers

■ Ambassador Speakers Bureau

P.O. Box 50358
Nashville, TN 37205
Phone: (615) 370-4700
Fax: (615) 661-4344
Web site: www.ambassadoragency.com

■ Speak Up With Confidence Speaker Services

1614 Edison Shores Pl.
Port Huron, MI 48060-3374
Phone: (888) 870-7719
Fax: (810) 987-4163
E-mail: speakupinc@aol.com
Web site: speakupspeakerservices.com

■ All American Speakers

200 Alexan Dr.
Ste. 208
Durham, NC 27707
Phone: (919) 403-7004
Fax: (919) 882-9497
E-mail: info@allamericanspeakers.com
Web site: www.allamericanspeakers.com

■ Premiere Speakers Bureau

1000 Corporate Centre Dr.
Ste. 120
Franklin, TN 37067
Phone: (615) 261-4000
Fax: (615) 261-2108
Web site: faith.premierespeakers.com

Men's Ministry Organizations

This is a representative list of those that have presented their seminar materials at weekend men's ministry retreats—but it isn't an exhaustive list of parachurch men's ministry organizations.

■ Man in the Mirror

180 Wilshire Blvd.
Casselberry, FL 32707
Phone: (407) 472-2100
Toll free: 1-800-929-2536
E-mail: events@maninthemirror.org
Web site: www.maninthemirror.org

■ Dad the Family Shepherd

P.O. Box 21445
Little Rock, AR 72221
Toll free: 1-800-234-DADS (3237)
E-mail: DadFamShep@aol.com
Web site: www.dtfs.org

■ Great Dads

P.O. Box 7537
Fairfax Station, VA 22039
Phone: (703) 830-7500
Toll free: 1-888-GRT-DADS
Web site: www.greatdads.org

■ On Target Ministries

P.O. Box 1654
Monument, CO 80132-1654
Toll free: 1-800-367-6364
E-mail: info@otm.org
Web site: www.otm.org

■ A Chosen Generation

PMB #355
11757 W. Ken Caryl Ave. F
Littleton, CO 80127
Phone: (303) 948-1112
E-mail: info@achosengeneration.org
Web site: www.achosengeneration.org

TOOLBOX
Organizations

■ The National Center for Fathering

P.O. Box 413888
Kansas City, MO 64141
Phone: (913) 384-4661
Toll free: 1-800-593-DADS
E-mail: dads@fathers.com
Web site: www.fathers.com

■ Character That Counts

1440 S.W. Jefferson
Lee's Summit, MO 64081
Phone: (816) 525-6339
E-mail: info@characterthatcounts.org
Web site: www.gospelcom.net/ctc/indexframes

TOOLBOX
Budget

Building a Retreat Budget

Speaker _____

Honorarium _____

Travel _____

Hosting/accommodations _____

Facility _____

Rental fees _____

Insurance (liability) _____

Meals _____

Snacks _____

Recreation fees _____

Audiovisual rental _____

Other equipment rentals _____

General items _____

Printing _____

Promotion costs _____

Miscellaneous _____

Contingency _____

Men's Retreat Promotion Timeline

6 months

☐ Complete planning stage.
☐ Make a "save the date" announcement.

5 months

☐ Design posters.

4 months

☐ Get posters printed.
☐ Design video/PowerPoint announcements.
☐ Write and design retreat brochures.
☐ Create bulletin-insert fliers.

12 weeks

☐ Put up posters.
☐ Record video announcement.
☐ Have retreat brochure printed.
☐ Print and insert bulletin fliers.

10 weeks

☐ Present live interview or testimony during church services.
☐ Mail brochures.

8 weeks

☐ Show video announcement.
☐ Write phone-call script.

5 weeks

☐ Show video announcement (during church services and/or at registration table in church foyer).
☐ Recruit phone volunteers.

4 weeks

☐ Present live interview or testimony during church services.
☐ Begin phone-call campaign.

3 weeks

☐ Continue phone-call campaign, if necessary.
☐ Repeat video announcement.

2 weeks

☐ Announce reminder during church services.
☐ Repeat video announcement.

1 week

☐ Show video announcement.
☐ Follow up with "It's last minute but not too late" announcement.

3 days

☐ Finalize registration list.

Retreat weekend

☐ Record video for next year's promotional use.

1 week after

☐ Hold meeting to evaluate promotion successes, failures, and desired improvements.

4 weeks after

☐ Turn in promotion task force materials to chairman for creating/updating operations manual

8 weeks after

☐ Set date for next year's retreat.
☐ Make early "save the date" announcement.

TOOLBOX

Retreat Follow-Up Survey

1. Is this your first men's ministry retreat?

2. What did you like most about the retreat?

3. What did you like least about the retreat?

4. What could be improved?

5. Are you willing to serve on a task force to help put on next year's retreat?

6. Did the speaker address your needs?

7. Do you believe the speaker's topics were relevant to the men who attended?

8. How was the praise and worship time helpful to you?

9. Were the recreational opportunities on target?

10. Did you have enough free time at the event?

TOOLBOX
Follow-up Survey

11. On a scale of 1 to 10 with 10 being perfect
and 1 totally unacceptable, rate the following:

_____ Accommodations

_____ Food

_____ Music

_____ Speaker

_____ Recreation

_____ Promotion of the event

_____ Small groups/breakout sessions

_____ Overall setting

_____ Impact on your life

_____ Opportunity to grow spiritually

_____ Opportunity to build relationships with other men

_____ Opportunity to relax and enjoy a change of pace

Finally, feel free to share any specific or general comments about the
event.

GET MEN TO REACH OUT

Outreach: Stepping Out of Your Comfort Zone

by Eric T. Rojas

Chapter summary: How to keep your men's ministry going and growing by reaching out beyond your church walls.

OUTREACH: STEPPING OUT OF YOUR COMFORT ZONE

One Sunday after one of our church services, I was walking down the aisle headed toward our lobby. All of a sudden, Sam—a big, burly, three-hundred-pound-plus man—slapped me on the back and said, "Hey, I know you!"

Even though I was standing in my own church, a wave of fear shot through my body. This man wasn't just large; he was ominous looking as well. He was obviously a biker—with tattoos, a bushy graying beard, dark sunglasses, earrings on top of earrings, and dressed in black leather.

Nervously, I replied, "Where do you know me from?"

"I saw you up front at that baseball deal last February," Sam said, "and I wanted to let you know how much that changed my life."

He was referring to an outreach event our men's ministry had held with a former baseball star. Apparently, Sam had attended. He said, "That night, I accepted Christ as my Savior and now I'm a new man—living the best I can and making changes to be God's man. I live quite a ways from here now, but I wanted to let you know how thankful I am for that night."

When a man commits his life to Christ, he can impact the world with an incredible, life-changing, culture-altering resolve. You probably agree with the importance of reaching men for the sake of Christ. Jesus modeled the ministry of reaching men who in turn reach their families and spheres of influence. Certainly, it isn't all that Jesus did or all that we should do. But we should place a primary ministry value on reaching out to men.

Reaching out to men is a difficult ministry. They're hard to reach, difficult to persuade, and grueling to develop. But so is marriage, raising kids, running a business, coaching a sports team—and we don't seem to be running from those challenges. OK, some people do run from those things, but anyone truly committed doesn't run. In the church, we shouldn't run away from the challenge of outreach to men either.

What Is Outreach?

Let's begin our discussion of outreach with this question in mind: What are we trying to accomplish with "outreach"? The story of Sam, the biker guy, contains one of the most natural meanings of outreach: providing an opportunity to share the message of the gospel with people who don't know Christ. But let's expand on that.

Outreach 1: Using any means possible to share the message of the gospel through *presenting or proclaiming* it to those who *don't have a personal relationship* with Christ. First Corinthians 9:22b says, "I have become all things to all men so that by all possible means I might save some."

Outreach 2: Using any means possible to share the message of the gospel through *serving* those who are in need *whether or not they have a personal relationship* with Christ. "If anyone has material possessions and sees his brother in need but has no pity on him, how can the love of God be in him?" (1 John 3:17).

The first type of outreach typically occurs in three ways: (1) at a one-time outreach event, (2) as an on-going outreach ministry, and (3) through personal outreach conversations and relationships.

All of these methods are valid and valuable. To reach men for Christ, you must be willing to reach them where they are, when they're there, and with whatever means possible to get them where they need to go. Using a one-time outreach event can be a great tool for a man who has difficulty sharing his faith with others, or it can open a door to a spiritual conversation you've never been able to have before.

Having an ongoing outreach ministry lets the men of your church know that there are ongoing evangelism opportunities through the church that they can make use of to reach their friends, co-workers, and neighbors.

At the same time, we should never be so concerned with events and programs that we're not personally sharing our faith and not encouraging and equipping others to do the same.

The second type of outreach is equally as important. This involves service through the network of communities that men are connected to. It means equipping men to serve others and reach out with the love of Christ. This occurs first to the community of family and friends in a man's life, then within his church family, then in the community where he lives, and finally, throughout the world.

The goal of this section is to help your men's ministry accomplish effective outreach to your communities of influence through both evangelistic and service efforts. We'll look at how-to's, ideas, strategies, and programs that can help your ministry right away and for years to come. While churches of different sizes will have different resources available to them, the principles of reaching out to men are the same.

Keeping the Main Thing the Main Thing

One of the most enduring jokes (or truths!) about men is that we're notorious for not stopping for directions when we're lost. A close second is that we won't read directions when we're assembling something. When it comes to ministry to men, we need to do both—stop for directions and read the directions. We're simply not smart enough, and we can't work hard enough to make this "men's thing" work. We're in desperate need of God's counsel through prayer and through his Word—prayer and Bible study are the most practical and basic practices that any man of God and leader of men needs to develop.

Before you skip over these words because you "already know that," hear me out. We live in a culture where nearly all people say they believe in God. Yet a relative few actually live out their beliefs. So here's a question for you as a leader of men's ministry: Certainly, you believe that prayer and God's Word are important to becoming a man of God and ministering to men, but are you truly living it out?

Practically speaking, here are some things you can do to keep the main thing the main thing in your ministry to men.

- Develop a personal quiet time that includes Scripture reading, Bible memory, and prayer for yourself and for those in your life.

- Develop a regular time to pray for the men that you're ministering to and with.

- Develop a regular time to pray and connect with the men that you're personally reaching out to.

- Personally pray for events, programs, ministries, or service projects that you're developing.

- Recruit a team of men who will pray for the men's ministry and men you're associated with.

Knowing Men

The next practical thing to remember is that you must know men—how they think, how they act, how they're challenged. Men aren't the sex-crazed, sports-driven, money-hungry, power-crazed lunatics that the world makes us out to be. Well, some of them are; but they're only acting out what's been modeled and taught to them. It's your job to meet men where they are by understanding them, connecting with them through quality ministries, and challenging them to a new life of purpose, character, faith, and leadership.

Ten Key Values for Men's Outreach

Having a solid outreach ministry with your men requires some basic values and components in your overall ministry to men. Without these key building blocks, your outreach ministry won't get off the ground. Following are ten key values your ministry needs to accomplish successful outreach to men.

1. Determine Your Purpose

What's your plan, vision, or purpose for what you're doing and where you're going as a men's ministry? This is the "so what?" to your events, planning, and communication. Many men have attended pancake breakfasts, bowling nights, small groups, or men's retreats without any idea of why they were there or what was to be accomplished. Many times, guys don't know because the leadership hasn't thought it through—the men's ministry held the pancake breakfast and retreat because they were on the calendar and they'd always been done. But men want purpose, understanding, and a vision of where you're taking them. Let them know where they're going, and they'll jump on board and carry your ministry forward.

2. Gain Pastoral Support

If your senior pastor isn't on board with what your men's ministry is trying to accomplish, the obvious question is, why? Certainly he (or she) would love to reach men. And he knows the struggles that affect men. So why wouldn't he support a men's ministry? I'll suggest two reasons. First, he thinks it will be more work for him in his already busy schedule. Second, he's not sure what you'll do or if it will be done well.

To put his mind at ease, set up a meeting with him. Share the vision the Lord has placed on your heart for the men of your church and beyond into the community. Tell him about the leaders you have working with you. Invite him to be the main speaker at an upcoming event for the men of the church. Or ask him to be involved in a brainstorming session for an outreach event you're planning. Encourage him to share prayer requests with your men's prayer team. Let him know that you need his support but that you have no desire to increase his workload—just to involve him in key ways that support the overall ministry of the church. Even mentioning your events in announcements or things as simple as the men's ministry as a pastoral prayer item demonstrates support.

3. Communicate Your Vision

Use whatever resources you have to communicate the vision or purpose for your men's ministry. Produce a flier for the men of your church, an informational piece that allows men to see the big picture of what you're trying to accomplish. For each event, clearly delineate and communicate the goal of that event, as well as how it fits into the ministry's overall vision.

At my church, many of the events in our men's ministry are geared toward outreach. One spring just a few months after a big men's outreach event, we held our first men's Power Breakfast. The purpose of the breakfast is to build up the prayer life of the men of our church. At this first Power Breakfast, we didn't communicate our vision very well. One guy who loves making connections with unchurched men came that morning with a friend who'd never stepped foot in church before. They sat in the front row. This would have been great if it had been an outreach event, but it wasn't. That morning our pastor spoke on prayer and fasting. While I believe that God's Word never returns void, that man has never returned to our church.

The lesson? Communicate your vision clearly, regularly, repeatedly, and in as many ways as possible.

4. Pursue Excellence

The days when a man will settle for mediocrity at church are over—particularly if you want him to reach out to his network of relationships. He will probably survive another church service with Aunt Sally playing the organ with her mittens on, but he will come alone or with his family—that's it. You won't see him inviting unchurched friends to join him. Also, if you get a man to a place of service—where he's reaching out to the community—you need to deliver. If he finds that you're unorganized and unprepared and really don't care about his time or needs, he won't be back. One of the best ways to pursue excellence is to do what you can do in an excellent manner that glorifies God. If you can't do something well, don't pursue it until you can do it with excellence.

5. Do Guy Stuff

Have men's stuff at your events. Men's ministry should be fun. Men like to have fun. Make things fun for them. Use camping, sports, business, tournaments, speakers, paintball, movies, and any other appropriate means to reach them. Yet don't be afraid to talk about where most guys are in life. Talk about business, sex, money, marriage, relationships, power, and accountability. Don't be afraid to put the "man" back into men's ministry.

6. Use Tools

Men use tools every day at home, at work, and at play. Whether it's a lawn mower to cut the grass, a Palm Pilot to organize the day, or a softball bat to get a hit, tools make the man. Tools make the men's ministry, too. Men use tools to help them get ahead. Anything you can do to provide excellent and useful tools will go a long way to improving your ministry and connecting with men. Keep this in mind as you plan small groups, spiritual growth and leadership training, outreach events, and service projects.

7. Issue a Challenge

Why will two grown men still arm wrestle when given the chance? Why do companies create sales goals? Why do we make New Year's resolutions and set goals for ourselves? It's the challenge. Most men love and need to be challenged. Don't soft-shoe with men about their spiritual growth or their need to step up to the plate when it comes to reaching out to other men. Challenge their excuses. Challenge them to invest in relationships. Challenge them to dream big and to dare to live out God's purposes for themselves, your men's ministry, and reaching other men for Christ.

8. Create Community

Outreach will happen best when the men of your church create a structure of men's community to encourage each other, pray for lost friends, hold one another accountable, reach out to unchurched friends, and study the Bible's teaching on reaching out. One of the best ways to accomplish community is in men's small groups. If you've tried small groups, and they didn't work, then try something else. However, keep in mind that true community must be intimate. Jesus had twelve friends (the disciples), and within that group he had three close friends (Peter, James, and John). Always keep in mind that the larger the men's group, the shallower the relationships will likely be, including the levels of trust, openness, and conversation among the men. Also, true accountability, challenge, application, and men's community can't happen in a mixed-gender setting.

9. Battle With Prayer

The book of Ephesians tells us that our battle isn't against flesh and blood but against the powers of the evil world. This is certainly true where outreach is concerned. There is one who hates the fact that you're trying to change men's lives and the lives of others. The key to winning the battle is to fight it on your knees.

For example, when you think about putting together outreach events, you quickly realize that there's a lot of work to be done! You need to plan the programming and promoting, figure out the logistics, pull together all the details, and follow up afterward. When you think it through, it can become overwhelming. Go to battle in prayer:

- Realize that God wants your anxiety: "Cast all your anxiety on him because he cares for you" (1 Peter 5:7).

- Don't do it alone. Gather your leaders and prayer warriors, and pray regularly for all aspects of the ministry.

- Watch for—even be amazed at—how the Lord moves and works in you and through you to change the lives of men through prayer.

Most of us struggle with finding the time to pray. The story is told of Martin Luther thinking about the coming events of his day. If it were us, we'd say, "I have so much to do today, I must skip my prayer time." But in the story, Luther said, "I have so much to do that I shall spend the first three hours in prayer." Focusing on outreach can be overwhelming, but through prayer, outreach can be more successful then you ever dreamed possible.

10. Pursue God's Word

While there's nothing wrong at all with reading books and using other resources to inspire and train the men in your ministry, one of the most important things you can do is to encourage them to pursue God's Word. Encourage it. Teach it. Model it. Apply it. Be about helping men get into the Word and use it in their lives. Consider these benefits of getting men into the Word of God (and this certainly isn't an exhaustive list):

- They grow to know God and Christ better.

- They learn the discipline of being a continual learner.

- Their goals for life are significantly transformed by God's Word.

- They gain power to fight temptations.

- They grow in their desire to reach out in service.

- They increase their ability and desire to share the gospel.

- They accumulate tools to become purposeful fathers and husbands of faith.

- They develop God-honoring leadership and character to help them in every aspect of life.

- They set an example for others in where to turn for comfort and guidance.

- They learn the heart of God so that he can transform their hearts.

- They see how to be part of something significant from an eternal perspective.

Training and Equipping for Outreach

We've defined what outreach is, looked at having a vision for outreach, and discovered the personal and ministry values to accomplish effective outreach. By now, you're ready to get to the nitty-gritty of *doing* outreach. But before you put on your first outreach program, event, or ministry, you need to equip and train as many men as possible with the how-to's of evangelism. Here are a few things to keep in mind.

- If your church or ministry hasn't found resources to use for training, look for training materials that work well in your ministry setting. There are many excellent tools that God is using to expand his kingdom. Our church uses the book *Becoming a Contagious Christian* by Bill Hybels for outreach training. And we use *The Church of Irresistible Influence* by Robert Lewis for service outreach training. While outreach can happen without training and tools, it will probably be harder and take longer to accomplish your goals.

- Provide the opportunity for men to go through whatever training you've chosen at strategic times a few months prior to each outreach event. Be sure to provide practical information on how to (1) extend invitations to outreach events, (2) start spiritual conversations, (3) share their own faith stories, (4) talk through questions they might encounter, (5) pray with those who wants to receive Christ, and (6) follow-up and disciple people within your ministry's guidelines.

- Realize that you can't train everyone. But God can still use untrained and unequipped men to accomplish his purposes. Don't get discouraged if a smaller number of participants seek training than you'd hoped for. Your role is to make sure you have the best tools to equip, the best time to train, the best teachers to present, and the best promoters to recruit. Let God take care of the rest.

Nineteen Steps to a Life-Changing Outreach Event

Now that we have laid the necessary groundwork, let's get to that nitty-gritty you've been waiting for. First, we'll look at nineteen things that you need to make sure you have a successful outreach event. Then we'll list a number of outreach events that can work for your men's ministry.

1. Study for the Right Event

Every church and every men's ministry needs to establish what will work where they are. While we'll list some successful events and ideas later, you must be discerning and understanding of what will work in your setting.

Begin by asking yourself, What kind of event would I bring an unchurched friend to? Dream out of the box—dream as if money and resources weren't a concern. Then talk to trusted guys in your ministry, and ask them the same question. Ask what types of events, speakers, music, and activities their unchurched friends would consider coming to if it was held at the church or sponsored by the church.

Part of discovering the right event also includes getting ownership both in your men's ministry and in your whole church. Ask church leaders if you can do a church-wide survey. Proverbs 15:22 states, "Plans fail for lack of counsel, but with many advisers they succeed." A survey provides a number of benefits:

- Men in your church will start getting excited about the potential event.

- They'll provide you with much-needed information, perspective, and ideas.

- They'll later feel ownership of the event, knowing they had a hand in creating it.

- They'll supply other ideas for future evangelistic events.

Do your homework. A successful event will speak to men where they are and address topics that concern them. Don't jump in too quickly. Before you make a final decision, take it to the streets. Ask some trusted guys outside your church—perhaps neighbors, men at your health club, or dads you meet at your children's school—what they might be interested in. Simply tell them that your church might host a community-wide event for men and you want to get their input. Most will feel honored that you thought enough of them to ask for their input, and they'll definitely give you valuable insight.

2. Research the Best Time for the Event

Your homework continues as you turn to studying the calendar. Begin with your own but continue by examining at least five others.

- *Church calendar.* Make sure you're not scheduling a potential conflict with another major event at church. If you do, you'll weaken your pool of leaders, laborers, and "inviters." If you're in a larger church, you might not find an open spot on the church calendar—but at least stay away from scheduling against activities that would draw men away from your outreach or that would cause facility conflicts.

- *Annual calendar.* Stay away from holiday weekends or even whole seasons that might create conflicts (such as summer!). If you want to schedule an outreach event related to a holiday or a season, consider holding it a week or two before the actual calendar days. For example, hold a summer kickoff before the school year ends in your area or hold a Christmas-themed outreach in early December.
- *Local school calendar.* If local students have a long weekend due to teacher in-service training, don't plan anything that weekend because families might use the time to get away. Be careful about scheduling an event around the time of school graduations. Or if there's a big crosstown rivalry sports event, don't conflict with that date.
- *Local community calendar.* If your town has a community festival or celebration, avoid scheduling on those dates—unless you can arrange an appropriate outreach activity connected to the celebration. Imagine holding an event where all the men in town show up!
- *"Men's calendar."* What's that? Typically, it's the sports calendar. For example, stay away from Sundays in the fall (football games), Super Bowl Sunday, baseball postseason games, and basketball's March Madness.

One more thought about scheduling: While you may not like the thought of catering to the world's agenda, keep in mind the purpose of your event—reaching out to unchurched, worldly guys. You're not compromising your faith; you're simply being wise. God will certainly honor that.

3. Create a Rough Budget

Do an early estimate on what you think the event will cost, what you might need to charge, and how you can raise funds if necessary. Begin by asking what funds you already can tap for an event like this.

Make sure your men's leadership team is fully on board with you. Ask them to help you estimate what the event will cost. Involving other leaders will help you be realistic. You'll likely have at least one guy who will think, What if this doesn't work? He'll provide good reality checks along the way. You may have another leader who dreams bigger than anyone could imagine—without thinking of the limits of time or money. It's good to have both types of thinkers represented on your team. How do you decide which direction to go with budget? I've learned to place extra emphasis on the type of thinker that I'm *not*. You don't want to create a team of rubber stampers, guys who just go with the flow without some give and take. It's the give and take that will take you a long way.

When it comes to finances, be sure that you communicate regularly with your church leadership. You may need your church to pay some expenses upfront. But if you present church leaders with a detailed plan and maintain open communication with them, they'll be more likely to help out as much as possible.

Don't be afraid to think out of the box. In many churches, there's simply not enough money to do every ministry that everyone desires to do. Be creative when it comes to finances. Work within the guidelines of your church but explore all possibilities. Ask guys to buy tickets for the men they invite, ask potential sponsors (usually businesses) to donate some aspect of the event, ask church leaders if people from the church can contribute beyond their church offering to cover costs of the event. Be innovative when it comes to your budget.

4. Hire a Great Speaker

Research the best possible presentation for your outreach event. The type of event you choose to hold will dictate the kind of speaker you bring in. Just make sure that your focus is on your audience—the unchurched guys you're reaching out to. Perhaps you have an opportunity to bring in a tremendous Christian speaker, but you need to weigh whether a speaker known only in churches will draw in your intended audience. Instead, seek out someone whose name will be recognized by unchurched men in your community. If that's not possible, look for a speaker whose name might not be known but who has a title that men will recognize. If the first two fail, then look for someone whose story is so compelling that men will want to hear it.

When it comes to someone with significant name recognition, it might seem impossible that you can secure this type of speaker. But you never know unless you try. Perhaps someone in your church has a contact with a nationally recognizable figure that you're unaware of until you put out some feelers. At a more regional or local level, maybe a known athlete has a great message and is willing to speak at an event like yours. A local television anchor might also make a good speaker.

The next option for an outreach speaker is someone with title recognition. He could be a businessman, such as a company's CEO. He could be a personality from a well-liked radio station. Or he could be someone with a leadership position in a group or organization. These types of men may be harder to find because you don't see their names in newspapers, hear them being interviewed, or have speaking agencies go after them. But if God provides a lead for you in this area, go for it.

The third type of speaker is someone with a great story but without name recognition. Simply promote and connect the story to men. It may take more effort than simply tossing out a recognized name or the title of someone at a well-known company or organization.

As you're searching for any of these types of speakers, keep in mind some of the qualities you'll desire in any speaker that you use. First, he needs to exhibit a mature, growing relationship with Christ. Second, he needs to show fruit that gives evidence to that walk with Christ. Third, he needs to have the gifted ability to articulate his faith and conversion experience. And be sure he communicates his experience in words that unchurched men will understand and relate to. That's a lot to ask, but you can't ask any less. How do you find out someone's story? Start with research, and then request tapes, CDs, or videos that show him speaking. Require a personal interview with him in person or over the phone before finalizing an agreement. Ask some tough questions—make sure he understands what you're doing and the purpose of the event.

5. Set Objective Goals

Refigure your budget, and set realistic goals. Now that you've researched and thought through more aspects of the event, get some objective numbers down on paper. Put real numbers to what a budget would look like and some realistic ideas of how you'll get there. Get your best "money thinkers" involved in this process—people who'll ask the proper and hard questions and think through details you might have overlooked or skipped.

6. Get Church Leaders on Board

Get your pastor and church leaders to support what you're doing. Again, this certainly shouldn't be the first time that you've discussed the event with them. At this point, you may want to present a formal proposal for their input and approval. They will probably have some great additional ideas, and it gives them a sense of ownership of the activity. It also provides accountability and can help you make tough calls if you're dealing with an edgy topic or speaker.

7. Book the Event

Officially get your event on the church calendar and book your event's presenter(s). Make everything official. Sign a contract, and pay a deposit, if required, to your presenter. Follow up with a letter detailing any additional expectations you've discussed verbally. This also applies to other presenters—for example, a baseball clinic group, a comedy troupe, or an acting team.

By the way, if you are inviting more then one presenter or using an off-campus venue, make sure everything lines up before making the event official. If you have an event away from your church facility with a guest speaker and a guest music group, you need to make sure the off-campus facility and the guests are all available on the same date and time; also be sure that facility, speakers, and musicians will meet your expectations and requirements.

8. Plan Other Aspects

Now that you have your main presenter nailed down, what else needs to be done? It's easy to fall into the special event trap of having a meal, an introduction, a prayer, a joke or two, and then the speaker. While the presenter can make that evening a success, could it be better? Can you connect with your audience in other ways—through other senses? One of the things we know about humans—and most men are human—is that you connect with them in various ways. Can you add: active elements, interactive exercises, visual connections, musical ingredients, and intellectual stimulation? Think through the following questions to help with your planning.

- Can you add environmental elements or décor to catch guys' attention?

- Can you incorporate a drama to set up your speaker and better prepare men for the presentation?

- What can you do to get guys laughing? Allowing men to laugh will soften them up to hear the message and make the event more memorable and enjoyable.

- Can you introduce your presenter with a video or create a video that introduces the theme?

- What about music? Is there appropriate music that you can put together for this event? Make sure it's music that unchurched men would hear in their daily lives *and* that it's done well.

- Can you add anything before or after the actual event that can make it more interactive and community focused?

- Is there an opportunity to include a meal? If you can get guys around tables talking and eating and having a good time, some great interaction and community building will take place.

9. Establish a Timeline

At this point, you should still be at least four to six months ahead of the event. This would be a good time to list how you and your team (see the next step) will get everything done. See Toolbox page 220 for an "Outreach Event Timeline." This is just a guide; if you have more time to accomplish each step, allow for it in your timeline. It's also wise to recruit a couple of people to help you flesh out your timeline because you'll likely forget something.

10. Recruit an Event Team

After you've established the main elements of the outreach, develop a team to cover all the bases. Establish an event leadership team that has one or two point people for each area, including food, traffic, decorations, music, drama, video, and promotion. Then (depending on the size of your church) encourage each leader or co-leaders to develop teams of their own for their area.

11. Brainstorm promotion

Put as many brains together as you can to come up with ideas for getting information to your men and for helping them get invitations to their unchurched contacts. Personally challenge your men, and build anticipation toward the event. Their personal contact with friends will be crucial in establishing an outreach mentality in your ministry. Make announcements in Sunday school classes, hold informational breakfasts, send personal e-mails or letters, and sit in on men's small groups.

Use every means possible to make your promotional efforts catchy, flashy, educational, and informational. Create high quality fliers that your ministry's men can use as invitations. Be sure to include specific times, places, and a map to your location. You might also decide to do additional announcing and advertising in the community at large. We've found that radio spots and business posters work better then newspaper advertisements.

While promoting this event, make sure you challenge men and groups to step out in faith to invite other guys. For example, set up tables that seat eight, and pair up guys who are active in your ministry. Encourage them to fill up the rest of their table with invited guys from outside the church. This gives each man a goal.

If you're selling tickets, make the price much higher for an individual ticket than for a pair or group of tickets. If you want guys to invite an unchurched friend, drive that home.

One last note: If you're just starting to do outreach events or if you've had outreach activities before but you're trying to revive your efforts after some failures, realize that it may take an event or two to develop or re-establish trust with your men. If they've been burned before when they've invited unchurched men to a subpar event, they may need to see an event first before they'll trust you again. That's OK—prove to your guys that you're serious about providing a tool for them to reach their friends who don't know Christ. They'll wish they'd brought someone and will next time around!

12. Establish a Prayer Team

You'll recall that we talked about prayer as a key value for any men's ministry outreach event. Hopefully, your men's ministry leadership team and others that you've asked have bathed your event in prayer up to this point. However, as soon as you finalize the outreach, establish a prayer team just for this event. This group can pray for

- all the details leading up the event itself.
- guys that your ministry's men are trying to invite.
- the event as it occurs and for things to go as planned.
- God to use your presenter to reach unchurched men effectively.
- commitments made, follow-up, and discipleship efforts after the event.

13. Create a Follow-Up Procedure

How will men attending your event be able to communicate the decisions or commitments they make during the outreach? How can they get plugged into other parts of your men's ministry and into your church?

There are three traditional ways of making this happen:

1. Trust that God will touch unchurched men at the event and that the men who invited the guests will continue to work with them and that the men will let their guests know about other ministries of your church.

2. Use a follow-up card that allows men to mark commitments they've made or request additional information they want.

3. Direct men to a follow-up room during or after the event where they receive follow-up information on the spot.

For the second and third methods, you'll also want to establish a two- to four-week discipleship process to follow up as well.

Because of the "tyranny of the urgent" of putting on a first-class event, it's easy to overlook this step or just throw it together. Don't make this mistake. Be purposeful in what you do.

14. Hold a Kickoff

Announce sales of tickets. Distribute fliers and invitations. Ask your pastor to make an announcement from the pulpit. Place posters around the church facility. Use a video announcement. Perform a skit during the church service. Any way you can jump-start the event will raise the excitement level, create momentum, cast vision, and get your men mobilized.

15. Double Check Everything

In the final two weeks before the outreach event, go through your task list, check in with your leadership team members, and reconfirm arrangements with presenters. Use your timeline as a checklist. This may seem like overkill, but it's not. You'll be thankful you took the time and made the effort when you discover a significant item that you overlooked.

16. Establish "Day-of" Requirements

The big day is here! You will want to establish some "day-of" guidelines and requirements. The main things to keep in mind are making sure that your presenters arrive in town early and at your venue in plenty of time. Allow time in your day-of plan for unforeseen difficulties that are certain to arise! Make sure that all of your teams and their workers arrive early, as well. Don't forget one of the most important aspects of the day—have fun! This is an exciting and memorable day. Make the most of it.

17. Execute Event Follow-Up

If you've remembered to plan for follow-up before the event, then this step should take place easily. If you do not have the speaker ask guests to make commitments at the event, then do all you can to funnel guys into a next event. That might be a special sermon series at your church services, smaller outreach events, and new small groups that cover material appropriate for new Christians or those on the verge of making decisions about following Jesus.

Another part of following up is making sure that you express your gratitude to your guests, and especially to your fellow leaders and any workers they recruited. They're serving because of their heart, but your expression of gratitude will encourage them tremendously!

18. Celebrate and Evaluate

Invite your leadership team to a celebration party within a couple of weeks after the event is over. You deserve it. Your team deserves it. Celebrate the high points, and discuss together what you could do better next go-around. Giving men this opportunity for discussion will provide insight you would never get without asking.

19. Start Next Year's Planning

Once you've pulled off a big event, look ahead right away. Schedules book up fast, and the more lead time and preparation time you have, the better. Your team will also feed off the excitement and enthusiasm of the event you've just been through. You can never start planning too early.

Ongoing Outreach

Rather than one-time or big-event oriented outreaches, your men's ministry might be better suited to provide ongoing ministries and programs as part of your ministry. While these are generally smaller in scope and expectation, they can reach men in many different sectors.

■ Affinity Groups

Often these ministries center around a particular interest. For example:
- sports ministries offer a natural place to connect with a lot of men.

- seeker small groups can reach out to men ready to discuss spirituality and faith issues.

- Seminars on financial and business topics can provide regular opportunities to reach out to men who might not be interested in any other avenue.

See Toolbox page 222 for some additional "Ongoing Outreach Ideas."

The key to these ministries isn't a lot different than other outreach events. You want to remain true to the values discussed previously, make prayer a foundational aspect of what you're doing, and pursue excellence in what you do. Be sure to keep the purpose in front of your leaders—that these programs are intended to be for outreach. It can be easier for that vision to wear off or get lost with ongoing ministries. Proactively hold your leaders accountable, and make sure to provide whatever resources and support they need.

■ Community Service

Your men's ministry can also influence your community by helping men reach out past their own worlds and serving people in need. This usually occurs among four major relational networks that you can challenge men to tap into.

This type of service was very prominent in the earthly life and ministry of Jesus. When you look at his life, it was all about serving. Whether it was performing miracles, healing the sick, or washing his disciples' feet, he set the example for us to serve others. St. Francis of Assisi said, "Preach always, and when necessary use words." That mentality will frame a heart of service in yourself and in the men you serve as together you focus on reaching out to your natural networks.

■ Family and Friends Network

God doesn't call us to serve only unknowns and people in run-down parts of town who have needs. He first calls us to serve our family and our neighbors. When you think of equipping and encouraging the men of your church to reach out to their natural networks, the first goal needs to be the network of family and friends. If you think that your family or friends don't need anything, look more closely. Serve the people you love most, and you'll be demonstrating the love of Christ.

■ Local Church Network

In his great wisdom, God established a network of Christians that we're all called to serve: the local church. In addition, he provides each of us with gifts to use to serve the church. He could have set up our lives to be independent or to focus exclusively on our families. But he chose to set up local churches as a connection for Christians. In our men's ministries, we need to challenge men to reach out to and serve the local church. Teach, train, educate, encourage—whatever it takes to get men serving this community. Imagine both the transformation within the church and the influence on your greater community if all the men in your church willingly served.

■ Greater Community Network

Look around at your community. Where has God strategically placed you, your family, and your church? Where has he strategically placed other men and their families? Your calling is to serve your community, then to encourage, train, and equip other men to do the same as described in Ephesians 4. Are you making an impact for the sake of Christ in your greater community?

There are three essential questions you need to ask when developing a community-network-based outreach ministry. How you answer can make or break the effectiveness of your outreach ministry. Let's take a look at the questions.

1. What strategy will you use to reach your community network? You'll quickly discover a lot of needy and valuable people and organizations within your community. Unfortunately it's impossible to meet the needs of them all. Some ministries choose to provide one-time help to many different local organizations, believing they get greater exposure that way. Other ministries focus on one organization and place all of their resources there, thinking they'll make a greater difference focusing on one need.

You might start by choosing to work primarily with Christian agencies in your community; this will help ensure that you're working with organizations that have motives in line with yours. While you certainly can work with non-Christian groups as well, realize that they may have different spiritual motives than you do. You might think of this as more of a social service opportunity than an outreach ministry. For help deciding who to work with in your community, see "Five Criteria for Connecting With Community Outreach Partners" on Toolbox page 221.

2. How will you implement your strategy? In other words, Who will you serve and how will you get them involved?

One method is to have a men's ministry day of service. You can arrange a good number of outreach service opportunities for the same day. This makes for easier promotion and a larger group dynamic.

A second option is to use men's small groups to mobilize the troops. You provide options—potential organizations and projects that you check out in advance—and let groups choose for themselves the project they want to get plugged into and the people group they want to reach out to. This gives ownership to the groups.

You might want to conduct test versions of these methods to see which works best for your ministry.

3. How frequently will you reach out? With the busy lives we all lead, it's easy to both over commit and under commit when it comes to outreach. You want to challenge the men in your ministry to make community service outreach more than just an option, but you don't want to demand that they over commit to doing weekly projects either. Suggest that individuals or small groups in your men's ministry serve once a quarter, and then provide the opportunity to serve more frequently if they desire.

The key to community outreach is to just do it. Yes, it takes additional time for administration, research, communication, sweat, blood, tears, and vision. But the passion will come to every man who takes the community outreach challenge.

■ Global Network

Right now the world is "smaller" than it's ever been. Almost regardless of where we live, we know the needs and problems of the world, and we're connected to the world as never before. With international missions organizations offering short-term opportunities that can test men's mission mettle, you can encourage, support, and equip the men in your ministry to reach out to the global network.

How you accomplish this breaks down much like the greater community outreach methods. It's crucial to start by working with your church and its existing partnerships. This is most often the safer, more productive, and more responsible path to take.

Because of commitments—including financial, time, family— it's usually unrealistic to take your entire men's ministry group to an international outreach project. Instead, offer opportunities to individuals in your ministry, who will then form a group to minister internationally.

Challenge

Well, there you have it—a practical look at the whys and how-to's of outreach. I pray and hope that in your sphere of influence, you'll become a man of outreach. What does this involve?

- Take on the personal challenge of proactively reaching out to those who need to commit to accepting Christ into their lives.

- Lead other men to accept that challenge as well.

- Lead your ministry to organize outreach events where men in your church can make an impact for Christ by inviting their unchurched friends.

- Personally look for ways to reach out in service to the networks in your life—your friends and family, your church, your local community, and the world.

- Challenge the men in your ministry to use vacations, days off, funding, and other resources to serve people in need.

Jesus came "to seek and to save that which was lost" (Luke 19:10, King James Version). And in Matthew 25:40, Jesus tells us, "Whatever you did for one of the least of these brothers of mine, you did for me." These are the simple goals of incorporating outreach into your men's ministry. May God bless your men as they reach out to others with the love of Christ.

Eric Rojas

Eric Rojas is the adult and men's ministry pastor at Christ Community Church in St. Charles, Illinois. His passions are reaching men, sports of all kinds, cheering on the Cubs, and spending time with his family. Eric and his wife, Rachel, have three children.

Visit his Web site at: www.ccclife.org.

CHAPTER 8 TOOLBOX

Outreach Event Timeline

1. Research the best event possible (6-12 months out).

2. Research the best calendar time possible (6-12 months out).

3. Do your first budget guesstimate (6-12 months out).

4. Research the best presentation possible (6-12 months out).

5. Refigure budget, and set goals—(6-8 months out).

6. Receive pastor and leadership support (6-8 months out).

7. Officially book your presentation (4-6 months out).

8. Establish the other aspects of the program (4-6 months out).

9. Establish a timeline for the event (4-6 months out).

10. Recruit an event leadership team (4-6 months out).

11. Hold brainstorm promotion (4-6 months out).

12. Establish a prayer team (4-6 months out).

13. Ask leadership team to recruit its teams (2-3 months out).

14. Provide service training for teams (2-3 weeks out).

15. Establish follow-up procedures (2-3 months out).

16. Have a kick-off Sunday for tickets (6-8 weeks out).

17. Double-check everything (2 weeks out).

18. Allow plenty of time for your "day-of" requirements (team arrives 4 or more hours early).

19. Remember to follow up and write thank you's (within 1 week after).

20. Hold celebration and evaluation party (within 2 weeks after).

21. Begin planning for the next event—ASAP!

TOOLBOX

Five Criteria for Connecting With Community Outreach Partners

1. Do a thorough job of investigating the local outreach ministries in your community.

2. Ask the church if they want to work with you in partnering with one or more local outreach partners. The Men's Ministry might very well lead the church to this ministry arena.

3. Try to partner first with the organization that best fits the resources, abilities and passions of your men. Interview the directors and dialogue thoroughly about how the organization operates, what associations it has, what financial accountability it has, what the general and specific needs are, and other pertinent information that you want to compile. A good organization will happily supply you with this type of supporting information and will appreciate the scrutiny.

4. Start with one organization and when you are out of work begin new partnerships.

5. Be sure to communicate with each group you investigate and let them know your plan and reasoning for choosing a different organization first.

Ongoing Outreach Ideas

- Workplace support groups

- Three-on-three basketball tournament

- Seeker small groups

- Business leadership workshop

- Golf tournament

- Financial matters seminar

- 5K/10K run

- Business seminar

- Comedy troupe

- Leadership seminar

- Drama troupe

- Community service

- Sports clinic

- Recovery groups

the 1 thing™

that everyone craves.

that really matters.

that gets undivided attention.

that can transform your life.

that encourages pastors.

that will re-energize you.

that will bring you joy.

that will unite your community.

that brings families closer.

that frees you.

that gives you focus.

that answers the why's.

that means true success.

that eliminates distractions.

that gives you real purpose.

that can transform your church.

Discover how *The 1 Thing* can revolutionize the way you approach ministry. It's engaging. Fun. Even shocking. But most of all, it's about re-thinking what "growing a relationship with Jesus" really means. Pick up Thom & Joani Schultz's inspiring new book today.

EVALUATION FOR
Men's Ministry in the 21st Century

Please help Group Publishing, Inc., continue to provide innovative and useful resources for ministry. Please take a moment to fill out this evaluation and mail or fax it to us. Thanks!

Group Publishing, Inc.
Attention: Product Development
P.O. Box 481
Loveland, CO 80539
Fax: (970) 292-4370

● ● ●

1. As a whole, this book has been (circle one)

not very helpful
1   2   3   4   5   6   7   8   9   10
                                                          very helpful

2. The best things about this book:

3. Ways this book could be improved:

4. Things I will change because of this book:

5. Other books I'd like to see Group publish in the future:

6. Would you be interested in field-testing future Group products and giving us your feedback? If so, please fill in the information below:

Name _____

Church Name _____

Denomination _____ Church Size _____

Church Address _____

City _____ State _____ ZIP _____

Church Phone _____

E-mail _____